STAR TREK

SPOCK'S
LOGIC PUZZLES

THIS IS A CARLTON BOOK

Published in 2015 by
Carlton Books Ltd
20 Mortimer Street
London W1T 3JW

ISBN 978-1-78097-574-0

10 9 8 7 6 5 4 3 2 1

Printed in China

STAR TREK
SPOCK'S
LOGIC PUZZLES

BY TIM DEDOPULOS

CARLTON
BOOKS

contents

INTRODUCTION 12

CHESS 16
FUZZY LOGIC 17
BALOK 18
TRACTOR 19
THE FIRST DOOR 20
WARPED 21
HONESTY 22
DIVISION 23
INTUITION 24
POLYWATER 25
THE SECOND DOOR 26
INSTRUMENTAL 27
ROMULANS 28
THE BIGOT 29
2 = 1 30
OUBLIETTE 31
QUINN'S PARADOX 32
ALL IN A ROW 33
THE CHAIR LEG 34
SCIENCE 35

GALILEO 36

URISDICTION 37

THE THIRD DOOR 38

CHAINS.. 39

BLACKMAIL 40

NIGHT SHIFT 41

THE FOURTH DOOR................................. 42

CRATES 43

TIME 44

LIGHT 45

BI-PLANETARY 46

GORN 47

LAZARUS 48

STARDATING.. 49

CONTEXT 50

DETERRENCE.. 51

KHAN 52

PARADISE... 53

BOOKWORM 54

CAUTION 55

HERACLITUS'S PARADOX 56

PETER .... 5?
THE FIFTH DOOR 58
NINE LIVES 59
TRINITY... 60
BURNING BRIDGES .... 6?
HATS 62
THE BOWMAN 63
APOLLO... 64
TOURNAMENT 65
LLAP 66
REDJAC .... 6?
SYSTEM SHOCK.. 68
WHERE NOMAD HAS GONE BEFORE 70
STRANGE DREAMS .... 7?
THE PIRATE.. 72
MIRROR, MIRROR.. 73
THE SIXTH DOOR 74
ALL IN A ROW... 75
MUDD... 76
TEMPTATION... 78
TROUBLE... 79

GAME SHOW 80
LION 81
FAMILY MATTERS 82
GAV 83
THE PARTY 84
MILTON 85
THE SEVENTH DOOR 86
LIVING SPACE 87
LIVING TIME 88
AHAB 89
IMPROBABILITY 90
FIZZBIN 91
HYDRATED 92
CONTINGENT 94
POLYHEDRAL 95
ROSTER 96
THE EIGHTH DOOR 97
GALILEO'S PARADOX 98
DECRYPT 99
O.K. 100
PILLS 101

PLATO'S DILEMMA 102

DOHLMAN 103

LIAR 104

THE NINTH DOOR 105

BRIDGE 106

NEW DAWN 107

THE ROMULAN PROBLEM 108

THEA 109

FALSE ANGELS 110

CHILDREN 111

BRAINS 112

LIONNAIS 113

STRIP 114

DEEP NOTHING 115

THE TENTH DOOR 116

GEMS 117

FEEDING TIME 118

RELIABILITY 119

POCKETS 120

DEFIANT 121

YONADA 123

T'SENG 124
RAGE 125
THE ELEVENTH DOOR 126
PLAY 127
GRANDIOSITY 128
SPEEDY 129
SCALOS 130
BLACK AND WHITE 132
LAST PASS 133
THE TWELFTH DOOR 134
MEMORY ALPHA 135
ARDANA 137
LITTLE MINDS 138
FRICTION 139
PARANOIDS 140
ZARABETH 141
FINALE 142

ANSWERS 144
ACKNOWLEDGEMENTS 224

INTRODUCTION

Logic is the beginning of the pursuit for wisdom. It is not an end in itself. The universe is fascinating and often unexpected. Unthinking reaction can be deadly. If you intend to prosper within it, as I hope you all shall, then you will need to cultivate logical thinking. Thus, this series of exercises, drawn from my personal experience. Study them, master their implications, and your increased rationality will serve you well in the depths of space.

This process is often difficult for humans. You are chimerical beings, inclined to listen to emotion over reason, to respond rashly. In certain circumstances – and if you are fortunate – this can be to your benefit. After all, your species has survived to make it to the stars. But there is a cold truth to luck, which is that it will fail you, sooner or later. Acting impulsively without logically assessing the problem is like the historical Earth 'game' of Russian Roulette. You might survive repeatedly, but the time will come when you do not.

When the stakes are personal, poor decision making is regrettable, but ultimately both the responsibility and consequences are yours to bear. However, as an officer of Starfleet, it is important to always remember that the consequences of your actions can be much larger than yourself. A starship is an amalgam, a single structure whose integrity and well-functioning is absolutely vital to the survival of all those who call it home. The stakes aboard ship are usually far more than just personal.

Put simply, for a Starfleet officer, hasty errors can prove disastrous beyond the limits of your imagination. In some circumstances, a society may depend on your timely and effective action. Entire civilizations have been lost because of an error of judgment. I have seen the after-effects myself. This is not a trivial matter. The more you train your mind to think logically, the greater the chance that you will make the correct decision in a moment of crisis.

It is a common human misconception to imagine that a logical approach to life is dull, unrewarding even. Many of you assume there is something inherently different about Vulcans that suits us to such a path, making it bearable for us. This is simply untrue. Our use of logic is both trained and fulfilling. Allowing the mind to retain clarity does not have to mean losing all access to emotion. It can simply mean unshackling the consciousness from the tyranny of blind reaction. Be the observer of your emotions, rather than their slave, and you can be truly free to make your own choices. What greater reward can there be?

PUZZLES

CHESS

After Christopher Pike was promoted to Admiral in the Earth year 2265, I stayed with the *U.S.S. Enterprise*, a *Constitution*-class starship. The new captain, James T. Kirk, was himself newly promoted from his previous command, and I had been Science Officer on the *Enterprise* for 11 years by that point. It seemed logical that I would best serve Starfleet by providing depth of experience to a new captain as his First Officer. It was one of the best decisions I have made so far.

Jim was a mercurial young man, driven by his passions. I suspected the worst of him initially, but his ability to play a reasonable game of chess provided some evidence that there was more to him than emotionality. Perhaps your facility for reason is likewise evident. Let us find out.

Consider the following three statements. One: James is a better chess player than Montgomery, but he is not as good as I am. Two: Montgomery is a better chess player than Leonard, but he is not as good as Nyota is. Three: Leonard is not the worst chess player out of the five of us.

If statements one and two are true, then is statement three true, false or uncertain?

FUZZY LOGIC

The human mind is a most dishonest instrument. It is prone to excessive emotion, which in turn easily dominates its weaker facility for logic. Thus reason gives way to folly, which feels, to the human thinker, like wisdom of the most profound sort. Many of the greatest ills of human society come from this intrinsic imbalance – but, to be fair, so do many of its greatest triumphs. Many of my fellow Vulcans would find it difficult to understand, but properly harnessed, irrationality can produce true brilliance. *Properly harnessed*. Without a great deal of care, irrationality inevitably becomes wasteful and destructive.

On stardate 1312, the *Enterprise* received a distress signal from the *U.S.S. Valiant*, which had been missing for two centuries. Investigating, she passed out of the Milky Way Galaxy, and through a peculiar energy field which killed nine of the crew outright. The field affected Lieutenant Commander Gary Mitchell, an old friend of the Captain's, unlocking his psychic potential. Mitchell gained access to a range of extrasensory perception (ESP) abilities, including the physical manipulation of the ship, and it became clear almost immediately that these were growing in power at an exponential rate.

We then knew, from remains we had found, that the *Valiant* had self-destructed after researching ESP. I recommended strongly to the Captain that Mitchell be put to death whilst such a thing was still possible. My suggestion was rejected; the Captain did not accept that the death of his friend would prove necessary.

What type of flawed reasoning is this an example of?

ANSWER ON PAGE 146

BALOK

Balok was the commanding officer of the spaceship *Fesarius*, a curious vessel of a civilization which calls itself the First Federation. The *Enterprise* encountered him in deep space, and he wasted no time in establishing himself as hostile.

After some discussion of our supposed disposition, Balok announced that the *Enterprise* was to be destroyed, and gave us a grace period of ten minutes, so that the crew could make peace with whatever deities they worshipped. Navigation officer Dave Bailey, faced with the prospect of impending death, became completely irrational, shouting at the other bridge officers for not joining him in panic. He was duly removed from the bridge.

What is interesting about this, from my perspective, is that Bailey had fallen into another highly typical human error in logical thinking.

What was it?

TRACTOR

Whilst trying to evade the First Federation ship *Fesarius*, the *Enterprise* was dogged by a small pilot vessel which used a tractor beam to impede our movement. This vessel was, of course, being flown by Balok, the commanding officer – and sole crewmember, in fact – of the *Fesarius*.

Now, the pilot vessel was moving in a straight line away from the *Fesarius* towards what I suppose to be First Federation space, at a speed equivalent to around one half of the *Enterprise*'s maximum impulse power. The *Enterprise*, on the other hand, was moving in an extended arc, since she was accelerating as hard as possible at 90 degrees to the pilot vessel's movement vector. With the effects of the tractor beam hampering movement, acceleration was around one quarter of the impulse power. After several minutes of this tug-of-war, the pilot vessel's systems burnt out, and the Captain beamed over to it.

At that point, and to within a spaceship's length or so, who was further from the *Fesarius*, Balok or Kirk?

ANSWER ON PAGE 147

THE FIRST DOOR

There is nothing instinctive about the Vulcan reliance on logic. On the contrary, we were once an extremely emotional race, given to extremes of violence and brutality that would horrify even humans. It was the philosopher Surak who led us to the Time of Awakening, showing us that the way to escape the endless cycle of slaughter was through using logic to control emotion. Even so, it took us 1,500 years to become the society that we are today.

The highest attainable degree of logical perfection we know is the *kolinahr*, a ritual discipline requiring years to master. Through it, all emotion is finally purged, and pure logic remains. Few Vulcans attempt to attain such heights; the monastic life is not suited to most.

Back in the murkier years of our mental evolution, the process that would become the modern *kolinahr* included a trial of suitability. This was a stark test of logic – a labyrinth of chambers, many of them filled with a gas that produced instant unconsciousness. A wrong move meant disqualification from both the trial and the proto-*kolinahr* itself. The first room of the labyrinth contained two doors, each of which bore a notice. The novice was told that one of the notices was true, and the other a lie. The task was to open one door, and either progress or be banished. On door A, the sign said "There is safety here in A, and oblivion in B." On door B, the sign said "There is safety in one room, and oblivion in the other."

Which is the door that offers safety?

There is safety here in A, and oblivion in B

There is safety in one room, and oblivion in the other

WARPED

For this particular problem, I want you to progress as if each of a number of statements is true. This is not, in fact, the case. However, this is not an exercise in general knowledge, but in the processing of logic. After all the statements have been made, your assimilation of the logical chains will be tested.

1. Everything that is not ugly could be housed in Yeoman Rand's room.
2. Nothing exposed to radiation is ever quite safe.
3. Warp coils are always kept in the containment core.
4. Nothing could be housed in Yeoman Rand's room that is not safe.
5. Nothing that has been gilt-edged could possibly be ugly.
6. Anything kept in the containment core is exposed to radiation.

Could a warp coil be gilt-edged?

HONESTY

Whilst surveying the M-class world Alfa 177, the *Enterprise* suffered a transporter malfunction caused by an unusual native ore. The Captain was exposed to the transporter fault, which caused him to split into two versions of himself – one embodying his positive emotions, and one his negative. A most curious effect.

Fortunately, he was the only victim of this accident, and we were able to reintegrate him properly. Suppose however, for the purposes of this exercise, that all of the crew had been exposed. Segregating the resultant throng into groups with no more than one version of any given individual, you find that in one particular group, you have 100 people. You know that at least one of them is the positive version, and from any random pair of individuals that you pick, at least one proves to be the negative version.

How many of the group are positive, and how many negative?

DIVISION

It can be difficult to correctly imagine the impact of repetition, particularly when the effects of such actions are cumulative. Whilst some errors are constrained, by nature or happenstance, to have a small effect, others may build upon themselves – a feedback loop that can swiftly lead to extreme circumstances.

Consider the case of an arbitrarily large sheet of thin paper, a mere tenth of a millimetre in thickness. Divide this sheet into two equal parts, and stack them together. Then divide the stack in two again, and restack. After a total of 50 divisions, approximately how high will your stack be?

INTUITION

Logic and intuition do not mix well together. Logic is, by its nature, methodical. You ensure the correctness of your deductions by relying on the correctness of your founding principles. If you fail to consider every step in a chain of deduction, you will very likely be led astray. Intuition, on the other hand, is a pole-vaulter. It leaps to a conclusion, and stays there, insisting that the conclusion is correct. But insistence is no guarantee of accuracy. Backed up by thorough analysis and logical inference, intuition can be a very powerful aid, but it should never be assumed that an intuitive decision is automatically a correct one.

Consider the extremely simple situation of a triple coin toss. You take three identical coins, each marked on one side and plain on the other, and throw them into the air. Each one, individually, has a 50-50 chance of landing marked side up or plain side up.

There are only two states the coins can land in, marked or plain. Since there are three coins, it is certain that two of the coins will be showing the same face, whether that is marked or plain. The third coin then will either be showing the same face as the first two, or the other face, at a 50% chance of each.

So the chance of all three coins landing with the same face up is 50%. Right?

POLYWATER

Stardate 1704.2 saw the *Enterprise* at the disintegrating planet Psi 2000. We had been due to collect a scientific expedition, but found all the members dead. It swiftly became obvious that this loss was due to a local contaminant that inhibited emotional control. A number of the crew, myself included, were exposed to the polywater in question. Dr. McCoy was eventually able to prepare a counter-agent in time for Lieutenant Sulu to get the ship away from the planet's destruction.

During the earliest stages of the infection's control, there was a period when people were alternating between sanity and madness. This is useful, for it provides the scope for a simple test of logical acuity.

Imagine a group of crew members, both infected and uninfected. One of the uninfected is exposed, switching over, and in doing so equals the numbers of infected and uninfected. After a period, that same crew member is cured, along with a companion. There are now twice as many uninfected as infected in the group.

How big is the group?

THE SECOND DOOR

If the novice passed the first room of the maze of the proto-*kolinahr* test – and the majority did, of course – he or she faced a second test, somewhat sterner than the last. This was the way that the maze was structured. Each correct option led to another, harder trial, whilst incorrect options led to instant unconsciousness. The failed candidate would wake from this state to find themselves outside the training facility, clothed and with any personal possessions they had brought with them. They would never again be allowed to set foot inside. Although a novice could delay a decision for so long as they felt necessary without penalty, there was no provision of food or water. Eventually, indecision would prove its own means of failure.

For the second test, there were again two doors, marked A and B, each bearing a sign. This time, the novice was informed that the signs were either both true, or both lies. The sign on door A declared "At least one of these two rooms holds safety." The sign on door B said "There is oblivion in room A."

What is the correct way forward?

ANSWER ON PAGE 151

INSTRUMENTAL

Deduction is one of the most fundamental aspects of logical reasoning. But permit me to be more specific. By deduction, I mean the process whereby previously-verified propositions lead necessarily to equally factual conclusions. In other words, the inference of specific facts from general ones. All active stars are hot, therefore this active star is hot. One is less than two, and two is less than three, therefore one is less than three. Simple though they may be, deductions of this sort are the building-blocks of all rational thought.

It is important, therefore, that your capacity for logical deduction be as finely-tuned as possible. Not all deductive chains are trivially obvious to the untrained mind. Consider the following three propositions, for this question, to be perfectly true:

1. Many musical instruments use strings to make sound.

2. There are stringed hand-held instruments, and stringed keyboard instruments.

3. Some furniture also uses strings.

Given the propositions above, which of the following statements are necessarily true?

1. Musicians' chairs are stringed.

2. All stringed instruments are either hand-held or keyboard.

3. Some percussion instruments are stringed.

4. All keyboard instruments are stringed.

ROMULANS

There are many tales passed around the training colleges of Starfleet, from cadet to cadet. Some are gruesome, some humorous, some purport to be useful and some are merely fodder for idle gossip. One I am thinking of in particular, about a Romulan commander during the Earth-Romulan War, may serve some tutelary use here.

Like many other species, the Romulans have a degree of capacity for psychic ability. It is rare, but not unheard of. One morning, a Romulan commander was interrupted at his breakfast by a member of his security team's night shift. The individual in question, a scanner operator, was highly agitated. Having been given grudging permission to speak, the operator explained to his commander that he'd had a terrifying prophetic dream during the night. In the dream, Federation forces had sprung a trap on the Romulan vessel, emerging from a specific gas cloud to surround and destroy her.

The commander decided to pay heed to the operator's warning. As the ship approached the cloud in question, he ordered an extensive battery of weapons to fire. The Federation forces lying in wait were crippled in the reverse-ambush, and the vessel easily destroyed all her opponents. With this achieved, the commander summoned the operator – and had him arrested, blinded and set to work as the most menial of slaves.

Can you see a logical reason for this treatment?

THE BIGOT

On stardate 1709, the *Enterprise* encountered an intruder in the Neutral Zone between Federation and Romulan space. The vessel, a Romulan attack ship, had been ordered to destroy a number of Earth outposts. Not only was this event the first confirmed hostility between the two forces for over a century, it was also the first time that the two sides had sufficient technological prowess to actually see each other face to face, as it were. It was something of a shock for the human crew to discover that they appeared physiologically identical to Vulcans.

Lieutenant John Stiles, having been brought up by a family consumed with historical hatred for the Romulans, found their appearance particularly difficult to rationalize. During the encounter, the *Enterprise* was quite badly damaged, and I attempted to assist Lieutenant Stiles with the operation of the phasers. He had become quite hostile towards me, suspecting that my similar appearance to the Romulans meant that I had to be in league with them. He dismissed my suggestions out of hand. As a direct result, he was badly injured, and Lieutenant Robert Tomlinson was killed.

What was the logical error that Stiles's bigotry drove him to commit?

2=1

It is extremely important, in logical thought, to ensure the precise rectitude of your chains of deduction. If you fail to do so, all sorts of errors can creep in and quickly become magnified to the point of utter nonsense. As a case in point, consider the simple algebraic proof that 2 is equal to 1.

First, let x and y be both equal to 1. Thus:

x = y

Now, since an operation done to both sides of an equation keeps the equation valid, we can multiply both sides by x:

x*x = x*y, or

x^2 = xy

Furthmore, we can subtract y^2 from both sides, thus:

x^2 – y^2 = xy – y^2

Now the two sides can be factored out, so that $x^2 – y^2$ becomes $(x+y)(x-y)$, and $xy – y^2$ becomes $y(x-y)$:

(x+y)(x-y) = y(x-y)

Finally, we can simplify by dividing both sides by $(x-y)$, so that:

x + y = y

But x and y are both equal to 1, so:

1 + 1 = 1, or

2 = 1

Where is the error?

ANSWER ON PAGE 153

OUBLIETTE

The *Enterprise* visited the penal colony on Tantalus V, to investigate the ravings of a mentally damaged psychologist, Dr. Simon Van Gelder. The incident was interesting to me personally, as it was the first time I had attempted to perform a mind-meld with a human.

I mention the penal colony as a way of contextualizing the following thought experiment. Imagine a prisoner who has been thrown into a primitive oubliette with smooth stone walls. The top of the cell is unbarred, but unreachable, and used only for the meager rations of food and water that are thrown down every day.

Desperate to escape, the prisoner begins digging into the floor in hope of tunneling out. Progress is slow without tools and, after a few days, the prisoner examines his progress. He knows that the walls extend several metres below the floor level of the cell. Estimated calculation makes it clear that it would take him many years – longer than he expects to survive – to successfully tunnel beneath the walls and up to the surface. In despair, he abandons his attempt. Then a logical thought occurs to him, and he immediately resumes digging.

What is his plan?

ANSWER ON PAGE 153

QUINN'S PARADOX

I have mentioned before that intuition can be a dangerous faculty. Allow me to provide you with an example.

Imagine that you have been offered generous pay to participate in a physiological experiment into human tolerance. You are connected to a device that, when activated, causes you an amount of pain. Each time the device is activated, the level of pain is increased by an amount just small enough that you are unable to distinguish it from the previous activation. To compensate you for this, the amount that you are to receive is also increased, by a non-negligible amount.

There is a degree of pain so unendurable that you would not accept it for any amount of reward. However, each individual increase is unnoticeable. If the previous activation was endurable, then this next one will be too; if the coming activation is unendurable, the previous one would also have been so. Thus it would seem that there is no point at which it is rational to stop the experiment.

Is there?

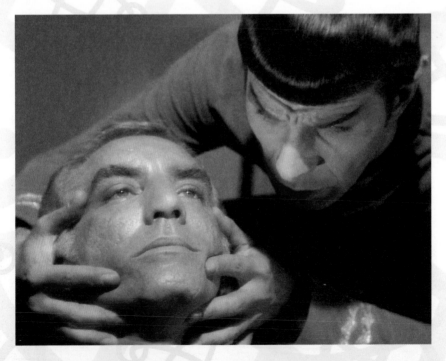

ANSWER ON PAGE 154

aLL In a ROW

On stardate 2713, the *Enterprise* followed a distress signal to a planet orbiting UFC 347601. Curiously, the star system was an exact duplicate of the solar system, with the third planet, the source of the signal, being a perfect replica of Earth as it was circa 1960. The human members of the crew found this extremely surprising.

It was later theorized that the entire system had been built by the Preservers, an extremely advanced alien species. As the Preservers have duplicated the planet Earth on at least one other occasion for the benefit of certain dying Terran civilizations, this certainly seems possible.

The planet we traced the signal to became known amongst the crew as Miri's World. Experiments in anti-aging had gone catastrophically wrong there, freezing the entire population at their existing age, but driving all adults into violent madness. By the time we arrived, some three centuries later, only eternal children survived. Full details are available elsewhere if the case interests you. For now, please consider this. The mother of one of the more mature survivors, a boy named Brian who typically wore an army helmet, had given birth to three children in total. Her first child was named April, and her second child was named May.

What was her third child named?

THE CHAIR LEG

Whilst exploring the remains of a ruined civilization on an exact duplicate of planet Earth, I distinctly recall observing Captain Kirk pick up a broken chair leg from the ground. He hefted it thoughtfully and then threw it away. The leg travelled a short distance, came to a complete stop, and then reversed its motion, coming back to his (fortunately) prepared hand. The piece of wood did not bounce, ricochet, or hit off anything, nor was there anything affixed to it. It was, in every respect, a perfectly regular chair leg and the laws of physics affecting the planet were identical to those of Earth.

I was not surprised by the leg's behavior, but more to the point, Captain Kirk wasn't either. Can you deduce what happened?

ANSWER ON PAGE 155

science

Repeatability is a vital part of the scientific process. If it is not possible to replicate an experiment, then there is no conclusion that can be safely drawn from it. It is, after all, vital that any deduction which is to become an accepted scientific fact be demonstrably accurate. If a theory does not account for observed local variance – say, for example, you can perform it successfully in one building, but not in another – then there is more work to be done.

For now, picture a situation where a scientist tells you that she is fairly sure about the accuracy of a certain theory. The results of her research have an 80% chance of being correct. Later, you talk to another scientist in the same field. He, too, has been testing the theory independently of the first, and he also feels that there is an 80% chance of it being correct. Then a third scientist reports that she has also independently calculated the probability of the theory's correctness at 80 per cent.

Thus you have three experts, each reporting that there is a 1 in 5 chance that the theory is wrong. So what is the actual probability that the theory is wrong?

GALILEO

En route to Makus III during stardate 2821, the *Enterprise* encountered a fascinating quasar-like formation designated Murasaki 312. We were in the process of carrying medical supplies for distribution to the New Paris colonies. However, the shipment was due in five days, and the journey time was just three. The Captain judged that the 48 hours that could be spared was sufficient time to survey the formation.

Myself, Dr. McCoy, Lieutenant Commander Scott and four other crew members were despatched in the shuttle *Galileo*. It was my first command, but events did not proceed smoothly. Ionization effects caused a crash on Taurus II, and fuel issues left us vulnerable to an attack by primitive humanoids. Two of the crew were killed. We were fortunate in being able to signal the *Enterprise* for retrieval during what would otherwise have been our last remaining moments.

The core point here is that issues of speed and time can be quite deceptive, even in relatively simple situations. Imagine that our journey into Murasaki 312 had been peaceful, and that we were dealing with petty units of speed and distance. If we had travelled 1,000 km at the rate of 15,000 km/h, how fast would we have had to make our return journey in order to average a speed of 30,000 km for the round trip?

JURISDICTION

The policing of criminal activity is a difficult matter even when contained entirely within one legal state. Faced with the complexities of interstellar travel, it can become extremely complex.

Consider the following theoretical situation. Alice is a woman who lives on planet Earth. Bob is a man who lives on Starbase 11. Whilst both are on the remote planet Gamma Canaris N, Alice attacks Bob, causing significant injury. Shortly afterwards, they both return home, and a month later, Bob dies as a direct result of his wounds.

Alice is clearly guilty of murder. But that murder obviously was not committed on Gamma Canaris N. Equally obviously, it was not committed on Starbase 11 a month later. So when was the murder committed? Some interstitial point? There is no court on Gamma Canaris N, so which location should have jurisdiction over the trial, Starbase 11, or Earth? Is there a logical solution which could form a general rule?

THE THIRD DOOR

As the trial of the proto-*kolinahr* maze continued, the tests of logic became tougher. Succumbing to tension was considered an emotional response, so if the pressure of the moment led to failure, that was proof of unworthiness in itself.

The third chamber was structured in a similar way to the former, with a pair of doors, marked A and B respectively. Behind each door waited either the way forward, or instant failure. Each door bore a sign, and the novice was told that in this chamber, the two signs were either both true, or both false.

The sign on door A read "Either this room holds oblivion, or the other room holds safety." The sign on door B read "Room A is safe."

What is the correct way forward?

CHAINS

Clear chain of command is a vital factor in any situation where strong leadership is necessary and there is a non-trivial risk of incapacitation or death. In its absence, confusion is guaranteed, and worse, there is a significant chance of some sort of power vacuum. For a military force, nothing is more deadly than a lack of leadership. Even a bad leader is to be considered superior to no leader at all.

For that reason, all ships, Federation or otherwise, have a clear line of seniority. On the *Enterprise*, I was the Captain's First Officer. Other officers in the command line for most of my time aboard the ship included Lieutenant Hikaru Sulu, Lieutenant Commander Barry Giotto, Lieutenant Nyota Uhura, Lieutenant Commander Montgomery Scott and Ensign Pavel Checkov. As enlisted specialists given equivalent rank, Lieutenant Commanders Dr. Leonard McCoy and Dr. Ann Mulhall were not considered to be part of the line of command.

Imagine we are aboard the *Enterprise*, and she comes under heavy fire. There is substantial damage, and I am killed outright. Lieutenant Commander Gary Mitchell has already died some time before. Who then would be in command of the ship?

ANSWER ON PAGE 157

BLACKMAIL

Consider, if you will, the strange nature of criminal law. In particular, I wish to have you think logically about blackmail.

Let us hypothesize that you know someone has committed a theft for which he is not under suspicion. It is almost certain that he will escape prosecution for this crime – unless you inform on him. If you were then to approach him and ask for favors, telling him that you will expose his guilt if he does not agree, you are committing the crime of blackmail, which carries stern punishments.

However, there is nothing legally wrong with approaching the same man in the same situation and just asking for favors. Similarly, there is nothing legally wrong about informing him that you will report his crime to the authorities. So why is blackmail a crime when its constituent parts are not?

NIGHT SHIFT

There was a brief, unfortunate period when I was required to seize control of the *Enterprise*, in order to deliver Fleet Captain Pike to the forbidden planet Talos IV. I am confident that Captain Kirk would have supported my actions, but the significant risk of subsequent execution made it illogical to involve him in my actions.

During that period, many of the ship's regular command routines were, out of necessity, disrupted. In particular I recall the helm as being significantly chaotic, both during my actions, and in the days following. As a consequence, several officers had to work quite unpleasant assignments. By the time normal routines had been restored, Lieutenant DePaul had worked more night shifts without break that Lieutenant Hadley, who had worked five. Lieutenant Kyle had to work fifteen nights in a row, more than Lieutenants DePaul and Hadley combined. Lieutenant Hansen had to work eight continual night shifts, fewer than DePaul did.

Can you discern the number of continuous night shifts that Lieutenant DePaul had to work?

THE FOURTH DOOR

The fourth chamber was the stage of the proto-*kolinahr* that started to claim a significant number of disqualifications. As in the previous stage, door A and door B were the only exits from the chamber, and each bore a sign upon itself. Either could potentially lead onwards into the maze, or to disqualification.

The instructions for the chamber itself were more complex than had previously been the case. If the sign on door A was true, then the room beyond it would definitely be the way forwards, otherwise it would lead to disqualification. If the sign on door B was true, then its room was filled with the knockout gas, otherwise it would lead onwards.

The signs on both doors were identical: "Both doors lead to safety."

Which door should the novice open?

CRATES

Imagine, if you will that you have three identical crates. One of these crates contains white balls. Another contains black balls. The third contains a mixture of both black and white balls. All three crates bear a label describing their contents, but in each case, the crate bears the wrong label.

For some arbitrary reason, you are not permitted to open the crates. However, you have an assistant who is permitted to remove one ball from one crate to show to you. Which crate do you sample to correct the labeling of the three?

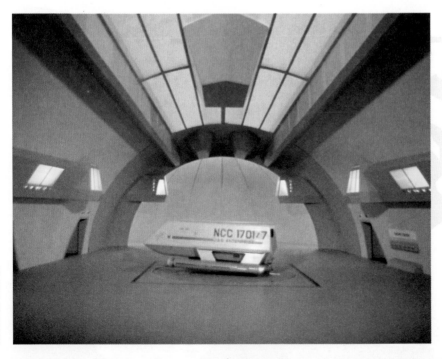

TIME

The correct measurement of time can be extremely important, as your quasi-mythical white rabbit would attest. It is quite possible that you may eventually find yourself in a situation where the passage of time must be estimated from just the most arbitrary equipment.

Consider an indoor environment where you are left without digital tools of any sort. You have a pair of lengthy, slow-burning fuse strings and the means to ignite them. Each will take precisely an hour to burn from one end to the other, but they are unevenly made, and you have no guarantee that any particular position on the burning fuse would mark any specific period of elapsed time since lighting.

Would you be able to measure the passage of precisely 45 minutes?

LIGHT

During my explorations with the *Enterprise*, I several times encountered planets with oddly anachronistic technology from the 20th century Earth. Sometimes this technology proved illusory, but other times it did not, and even the illusions were often convincing across all senses. So the following hypothetical exercise in logical analysis is not entirely trite.

You find yourself in a room with three switches, marked A, B and C. Each of the switches is in the off position. Through a door and down a short corridor is a second room, which holds an archaic, 20th-century style table lamp – the kind which provides light via a metal filament enclosed in a glass bulb. You are required, for reasons that need not be explored, to identify which one of the three switches controls power to the lamp. You are permitted to examine and even dismantle the table lamp, but the corridor from the switches to the lamp is one way. You will be able to move easily from switches to lamp, but you will not be able to move back.

How do you identify the switch that powers the lamp?

BI-PLANETARY

Let us theorize the existence of an Earth-sized planet, in a similar orbit to Earth around a G-type yellow dwarf much like Sol, and with a day somewhere around 24 Earth hours in length. So far, so Terran. However, in the face of all astronomical probability, the surface of the planet is solid and perfectly smooth to the micrometre level.

I feel I should step aside from the hypothetical for a moment to point out that I do not know of any perfectly smooth planetary surfaces. Even liquid-covered planets have ripples and waves, from tidal forces and/or atmospheric drag.

A pair of perfectly parallel train-tracks are built along the planet's equator, encircling it completely, and a pair of trains are set traveling around and around the planet on the two sets of tracks, one clockwise and one counter-clockwise, so that they complete one circuit of the planet each local day. They are dilithium-powered, with sufficient energy capacity to stay running indefinitely.

Assuming that the system is engineered so that the train wheels are the certain point of mechanical failure in the system, which train's wheels will wear out first?

GORN

Whilst in conflict with an alien aggressor of a species known as the Gorn, the *Enterprise* passed into the region 2466 PM. Unknown to us, this territory was claimed by a highly advanced species who called themselves the Metrons, who regarded our intrusion in the commission of conflict to be an unendurable insult. Their response was to move the Captain, and the commanding Gorn, down to the surface of a planet that they apparently prepared near-instantaneously just for that purpose. The two leaders were told that they would have to fight with just the materials available to them on the planet's surface.

During the contest that followed, Captain Kirk and the Gorn engaged in a game of cat and mouse, as each hunted the other whilst also assembling ad hoc weaponry. After the hunt was resolved, the Metrons further displayed their technological prowess by instantaneously teleporting the *Enterprise* more than 1,500 light years.

At one particular point during the contest between man and Gorn, the Captain was around five hundred metres north of a particular rock face. This rock face, in turn, was around 500 metres east of the Gorn commander. Would it then have been accurate to say that the Gorn commander was northwest of Captain Kirk?

ANSWER ON PAGE 163

LaZaRUS

Possibly the greatest crisis that the *Enterprise* ever faced was the direct result of an insane scientist named Lazarus. Improbably, Lazarus was a traveller from the distant past. He had come to the far future, to a time when his civilization was utterly forgotten and his home planet just a barren rock, in pursuit of a mortal enemy – himself.

As well as discovering time travel, his people had unlocked the secret of traveling to a nearby parallel dimension. Lazarus had become maddened at the idea of there being another version of himself, and resolved to destroy the duplicate. His efforts threatened not only the *Enterprise*, but both universes in their entirety. The threat was grave enough that the whole of Starfleet was put on Code Factor 1, invasion footing.

Whilst we were still endeavoring to make sense of Lazarus's initial claims of a terrible monster, I overheard him in a discussion with Lieutenant Charlene Masters. "Your captain has to help me," Lazarus told her. "If I fail, billions more will die." "I'm sure he'll come to the right decision," Masters assured him. "Either he gives me what I need, or he is in league with the monster," Lazarus declared.

What logical error was Lazarus demonstrating in that exchange?

ANSWER ON PAGE 164

STARDATING

Stardate 3113.2 saw the *Enterprise* thrown backwards in time more than 200 years, to 1969 on the Earth calendar. This is an excellent demonstration of the logic of adopting the Stardate system, incidentally – when physical laws are prone to warping under anomalous local conditions within the Galaxy, it becomes clear that absolute time and experiential time are prone to divergence.

Thus the Stardate, which both tracks relative experiential time for a given craft, and also reflects the conditions of the area of space that the craft is passing through. Although its calculation can be quite complex, computer automation handles all such details, and any given captain's reports thus become readily comprehensible. To further facilitate ease, the day is broken into deciles, rather than 24 Earth-hour slots. So at 3113.1, we were approaching Starbase 9 for resupply in the year 2267; by 3113.3, we were over Nebraska in the year 1969.

Consider the following fact. During the four-day period from 3101 to 3104, the *Enterprise* was either cruising or in orbit. On two separate days during that period, I played three-dimensional chess against Captain Kirk. Two of the days were spent cruising.

Given this information, which, if any, of the following statements can you be certain of?

1. The Captain and I played chess whilst in orbit at least once.

2. The *Enterprise* spent two days in orbit.

3. I won against the Captain at least once.

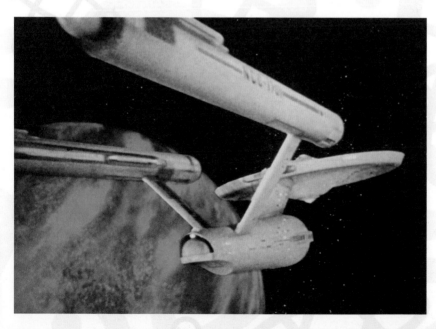

CONTEXT

Sometimes, the absence of context can be beneficial, clearing bewildering detail away to focus on the core issue. It should be remembered that just as often, wealths of detail contains information which is required in order to reach a logical conclusion, so be wary of reductionism as a universal solution. It is a tool, and particularly useful when your circumstances are proving problematic.

In this spirit, here is a logical trial for you that has been freed of extraneous detail. There are 20 small metal disks on a table in front of you. Each has been marked on one side with a fluorescent dye that is not visible to you under current lighting, nor is it ascertainable through any other option currently open to you. Exactly half of the disks are currently placed with the invisible mark on the upper side.

Your task is to divide the disks into two groups of ten, so that each group has the same number of disks with their marked sides upwards. How would you do this?

DETERRENCE

Sometimes, you encounter an enemy whose differences to your own are fundamentally irreconcilable. Where conflict seems inevitable, deterrence becomes important – but its usefulness is often deeply illogical, particularly when the threat you wield against each other has significant effects for both sides. Consider Earth history, and the insane spectre of 'Mutually Assured Destruction' that blighted the second half of the 20th century.

The trouble is this. Consider an enemy who wishes to replace your style of civilization with their own. You can only deter this foe by threatening to destroy both their civilization and yours if they defeat you – a deterrent in the model of your old atomic bombs. Your deterrent will only be successful if your enemy believes in your capacity to use it. But if they were to attack and defeat you, there would be no point left in carrying out your threat. It would be the most illogical action possible – to destroy the world, billions of innocent lives, merely because you personally have been removed from power.

Can a rational power ever effectively employ a devastating deterrent?

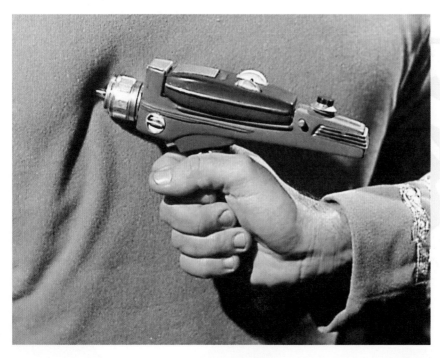

ANSWER ON PAGE 165

KHAN

The *Enterprise* intercepted an ancient Earth spaceship, the *SS Botany Bay*, on Stardate 3141.9. It turned out to house the human former tyrant Khan Noonien Singh, who ruled more than a quarter of the Earth during the Eugenics Wars of the 1990s. Singh and more than 80 of his fellow genetically-enhanced followers had fled Earth as the war ended, going into stasis as their ship fled the solar system.

The human crew of the *Enterprise* seemed to find Singh particularly fascinating, possibly because of some instinctive reaction to his forceful personality or over-developed physique. At one meal, I recall him claiming the virtues of his dictatorship. He specifically maintained that humans craved order and certainty. I suggested to him that perhaps freedom was a more basic human urge. He argued otherwise, on the grounds that every one of his followers agreed with him, showing that being benignly controlled was a universal urge in his species.

What logical fallacy was Singh demonstrating in that conversation?

paradise

The *Enterprise* arrived at Omicron Ceti III expecting to witness the planet's destruction, but instead discovered a flourishing colony. We did not initially realize that the colonists were infected with a local spore that induced a state of euphoric calm, as well as curing pre-existing illnesses, infirmities and even old scars. Naturally, the Captain expunged the spore from the colonists, and relocated them to a planet more suited to human truculence.

Assuming the following items of information are correct, identify the original technical speciality of the colonist who had previously borne a knife scar.

The textiles specialist had become a farmer, and was not named Leila, who had once had a bad knee. The colonist who'd once had lung scarring was an agricultural specialist, and was neither Michael nor Jeannie. The colony's teacher was not named Elias or Grant. The animal husbandry specialist had become the colony's crafter. The colonist who'd once had a badly-set broken nose was not a botanical specialist. Grant, who had once missed a finger, was not the colony's farmer. Michael was the colony's tiller, and had never had a knife scar. One of the colonists was the mayor, and another had previously specialized in medicine.

BOOKWORM

Before technology rendered them obsolete, printed books were very popular amongst the people of their time. I have never understood the appeal of nostalgic indulgence, myself. If something is obsolete and irrelevant, then it is obsolete and irrelevant. To valorize the outdated purely because it has become redundant seems the very height of human whimsy. However, I know that some people still value printed books greatly – my friend Dr. Leonard McCoy, for example, who has a shelf of over a dozen, arranged as tradition dictates with the spines facing out, for easier identification.

I will assume that you are at least familiar with the way in which a paper book works. On Earth, there were a number of insects that were prone to damaging books by tunneling through them, particularly the larvae of *Anobium punctatum*, the common furniture beetle. Like other so-called bookworms, *punctatum* was not drawn especially to paper, but to wood in general. Let us imagine that somehow, a *punctatum* larva infiltrated Dr. McCoy's shelf of books, and, further, that each book on his shelf was a standard ten centimeters thick, including cover. If the larva were to bore its way straight from the front cover of book one, the leftmost book on the shelf, to the rear cover of book three, how far would it have to travel?

CAUTION

The *Enterprise* crossed the path of Commander Kor of the Klingon Empire on Organia, a neutral M-class planet in disputed space between the Empire and the Federation. Our orders were to ensure the Klingons did not seize Organia as a base, as hostilities had re-erupted between the two civilizations.

As it transpired, the Organians neither welcomed nor needed our assistance against the Klingons. They were significantly more advanced than they appeared. Instead, they disabled our collective weapons, and imposed a new peace treaty on the two civilizations. Kor went on his way.

Of Kor's father, Rynar, it was said that he kept an honor guard of two at his sides at all times. These bodyguards were silent and unflinching, and stood a few paces either side of Rynar. Although they always looked straight ahead in opposite directions, without deviation, between the two of them they were able to always observe Rynar and his surroundings clearly. In this, they did not make use of reflective surfaces, nor of technology of any kind. How was this feat attained?

ANSWER ON PAGE 167

HERACLITUS'S PARADOX

Questions of space and time can strike to the fundamental limits of our understanding of the universe. Language rarely has the necessary vocabulary to clearly express those matters that science has yet to fully explore. To be faced with the truly ineffable can be an extremely humbling experience.

The archaic Earth philosopher Heraclitus famously stated that it was impossible to step into the same river twice. The gist of his argument was that a river is a body of water. However, before the second step is possible, the water that you stepped into the first time has swirled around, moved downstream, picked up impurities and so on. Even further, some of the river has faded away to become sea, whilst new water from springs and aquifers has bubbled up to replace it. It is not the same water, so it is not the same river. However, at the same time, it is clearly the same river – there it is, right before you, just as it was a few moments earlier. Hence the paradox; the river is both the same and completely different.

Is there a rational way to escape the paradox?

ANSWER ON PAGE 171

PETER

The *Enterprise* arrived at the planet Deneva on Stardate 3287. We were deeply concerned about the fate of the inhabitants. It appeared an outbreak of mass insanity had been spreading through the Galaxy in a straight line which fell directly upon the planet. The insanity proved to be caused by parasites. We were able to save much of the planet, but the Captain's brother, Sam, was amongst the casualties.

Human familial relationships are a matter of surprising complexity. There are many differentiations between the smallest nuances of heredity, of links by birth as opposed to marriage, of links between different generations, and so on. It is a highly illogical system, but obviously one to which you are significantly invested.

So, tell me this. What is the nearest, most direct relationship that the brother-in-law of your mother's brother could have to you?

ANSWER ON PAGE 171

THE FIFTH DOOR

As novices entered the fifth chamber of their trial of logic, they discovered that the true heart of the test was finally beginning. The first four rooms weeded out the deficient, whilst the next four eliminated the incautious. There was no allowance for error during our slow climb to genuine rationality.

As before, the fifth chamber held two doors, A and B, each bearing a sign either true or false, and leading to a room. Each room either led onwards, or unleashed instant unconsciousness and banishment. The candidate was informed that in this chamber, sign A would be true only if room A was safe, whereas sign B would be false if room B was safe.

Sign A declared, "At least one of these rooms is safe." Sign B said "The other room is safe." Which door should the candidate choose?

nine Lives

I was once exposed to a story passed down through human culture from the pre-Federation days of Earth. It provides some interesting tutelary opportunities, dealing as it does with a wide range of physical laws and related phenomena. My personal opinion is that the story is quite likely to be apocryphal, as it has an air of contrivance about it, but I do not honestly possess enough evidence for or against to arrive at a definite conclusion regarding the matter.

In the story, an entirely black cat steps onto a stretch of black road. It wears no collar, bell, or other devices or ornamentation. There are no street lights to illuminate its way, nor house lights. The sky is overcast, and there is not even the smallest glimmer of moonlight. The only vehicle on the road is a car, also black, speeding directly towards the cat – and its lights are all turned off, including side-lights and indicator lights. Nevertheless, the driver of the car deliberately slows down, and permits the cat to cross the road safely.

What alerted the driver to the cat's presence?

ANSWER ON PAGE 172

TRINITY

Picture the following situation. There are three guests at a party, people who are unfamiliar to you personally. One is dressed in green, another in gold and a third in black. You have been informed that the three actually are named Green, Gold and Black, but that none of them has dressed so as to match the color of their clothes to their own name.

Approaching, you hear the following snatch of conversation.

"It's a strange thing. Here we are, and our surnames and shirt colors form identical groups of three. Being called Black, I hardly ever wear clothes that color."

"It happens more than you'd think," replied the person in gold.

"I'm unconvinced," said the third.

Who is who?

BURNING BRIDGES

I once overheard Lieutenant Uhura teasing Lieutenant Commander Scott over a persistent minor problem regarding the functionality of the impulse drives. Something in one of the coolant systems was knocking and impeding peak power slightly. The cause seemed impossible to locate, and it was driving Lieutenant Commander Scott to a frenzy of impatient distraction.

Lieutenant Uhura, feeling mischievous, suggested that the problem was in fact being caused by a gremlin having taken up residence in the cooling system pipes.

"There's no such thing as gremlins," Lieutenant Commander Scott told her, clearly annoyed.

Lieutenant Uhura pressed on. "How do *you* know? Can you prove it?"

"What? Prove it? Of course not. You can't prove a negative."

"So it's gremlins, then. You just said so yourself." Lieutenant Uhura smirked at Lieutenant Commander Scott.

"That's not how it works at all," protested Lieutenant Commander Scott.

At that point, the Captain told them to stop bickering, which they did. What logical error was Lieutenant Uhura demonstrating in that exchange?

ANSWER ON PAGE 173

HATS

In this utterly contrived scenario, you are at the front of a short line of three people. You know that your companions in this line are honest, rational beings. Each of you is under strict orders to only face the front, so whilst the person at the end of the line can see both you and the person behind you, and the person in the middle can see you, you cannot see any of them.

Once you are in place, each of you have a small hat placed on your heads. You are informed, by your controllers, that your hats have been selected at random from a pool of five possible candidates. Three of these candidates are blue, and the remaining two are red.

The person at the end is instructed to say what the color of their hat is, if they know. "No idea," is the answer. The person in the middle is then given the same instruction. This time, the answer is "I can't tell."

What color is your hat?

THE BOWMAN

Captain Kirk, Doctor McCoy and myself were stranded on the planet Capella IV whilst attempting to negotiate important mining rights. Our situation was the result of Klingon intrigue, luring the *Enterprise* out of our orbit with false distress signals. On the planet's surface, we found ourselves in an extremely perilous situation without recourse to weapons. We decided to construct a primitive bow and some arrows for the Captain.

During the construction process, the Captain informed me of a legend of an old Earth hero. Apparently, this fellow was so skilled with a bow that, even blindfolded, he could be aimed at a target 100 metres away and still put an arrow straight through his hat.

The Captain seemed quite put out that I was not impressed by this reported feat, but surely you can see how such a thing is trivially easy?

APOLLO

Approaching Pollux IV, the *Enterprise* was halted by a gigantic hand of energy. Investigating, we discovered a humanoid being who displayed incredible powers, and claimed to be – and probably was – Apollo, one of the ancient gods of Earth. This individual wanted to use the ship's anthropology and archaeology officer, Lieutenant Carolyn Palamas, to breed a new race of gods who would spread out across the Galaxy. He also wished to keep the *Enterprise* and her crew as mindless worshippers, imprisoned on the planet.

Apollo was, of course, effectively destroyed, his power and sentience broken.

Later, I discussed the matter with the Captain. As it transpired, he and Apollo had discussed the matter of freedom versus servitude, leading to the Captain's conviction that the ancient being had to be stopped. The Captain had informed Apollo that freedom was a treasured right of mankind. Apollo replied that the Captain was insisting that humanity have the right to murder, pillage, betray, and slaughter according to its whims. Because of this, freedom was an abomination, and its absence should be celebrated, not condemned.

What logical error is Apollo committing in this discussion?

TOURNAMENT

On stardate 3372, certain medical requirements necessitated that I return to Vulcan for a period. Whilst there, Captain Kirk was manipulated into agreeing to a ceremonial fight with me. I was, I admit, quite satisfied to discover that despite appearances, I did not actually slay him in the end.

That contest puts me in mind of a less desperate Vulcan tradition where 128 participants strive to be the last remaining contender. Each match takes place between two people. The winner advances to the next round, with the loser being dropped from the competition. A draw situation is not possible.

How many matches does this contest comprise of?

ANSWER ON PAGE 175

LLaP

Ritual greeting exchanges are common in sentient cultures, regardless of species. When meeting a new person, a simple gesture indicating friendliness is one of the most effective ways of reducing the likelihood of violence, which can always prove catastrophic to the individual. Certainly, such a gesture can be a deception, but since the randomly violent seldom survive long, and plotting personal malice requires motivation and time, it is rational to assume that a greeting of peaceful intent will usually be honest.

Of course, it is just as true that, having become a social norm, refusing to engage in a greeting exchange can be a statement of dominance and arrogance. Imagine a meeting of 20 humans, no two of precisely identical heights. They are expected to shake hands with each other attendee, but if any given individual refuses to shake hands with someone shorter than they are, how many handshakes will take place in total?

REDJAC

On the planet Argelius II, the *Enterprise* came into contact with an extremely unpleasant and dangerous body-hopping entity named Redjac. This creature fed on fear, and had spent centuries terrorizing people. It's usual mode of operation was to possess someone, and use this poor, husked host to go on murder sprees, cowing the local population into perpetual terror. When discovered, it would jump to its next host and move on. We were able to defeat the entity, and eventually confirmed a series of planets that it had operated on, one after another, along with details about its hosts, and the weapons it used in each location.

The host on Deneb II worked as a dancer, whilst the host on Argelius II used a dagger, and the host on Mars was named Penny. The hunter, whose name was Beratis, was host immediately before the administrator. The host with brown hair used a garrotte. The host who worked as a surgeon had black hair, whilst the third host was named Kesla. The resident of Earth was the first host. The host with yellow hair fell adjacent to the host who used a scalpel, whilst the host with black hair was adjacent to the host who used a pickaxe. The host named Hengist was bald, but the host on Rigel IV had blue hair. The host from Earth fell adjacent to the host who worked as a miner. The host named Jack fell adjacent to a host with yellow hair.

On what planet did the host use a hatchet?

SYSTEM SHOCK

Following the *Enterprise's* encounter with the *U.S.S. Constellation*, a near-derelict ship of the *Constitution* class, we took significant damage. We were forced into hazardous confrontation with a gigantic intergalactic weapon, which I suspect to have been a relic of some long-dead species. Following the encounter, several of the *Enterprise's* core systems were unreliable for a period of time.

During that period of time, I observed that in any given decile of a day, if the transporter was broken, the warp engines were online, whilst if the warp engines were disabled, the transporter was functional. One of the two systems was malfunctioning in nine deciles in total during the period, whilst the transporter was functional during six deciles, and the warp engines functional during seven deciles.

What is the smallest amount of time, in deciles, that this observed period of instability could have lasted?

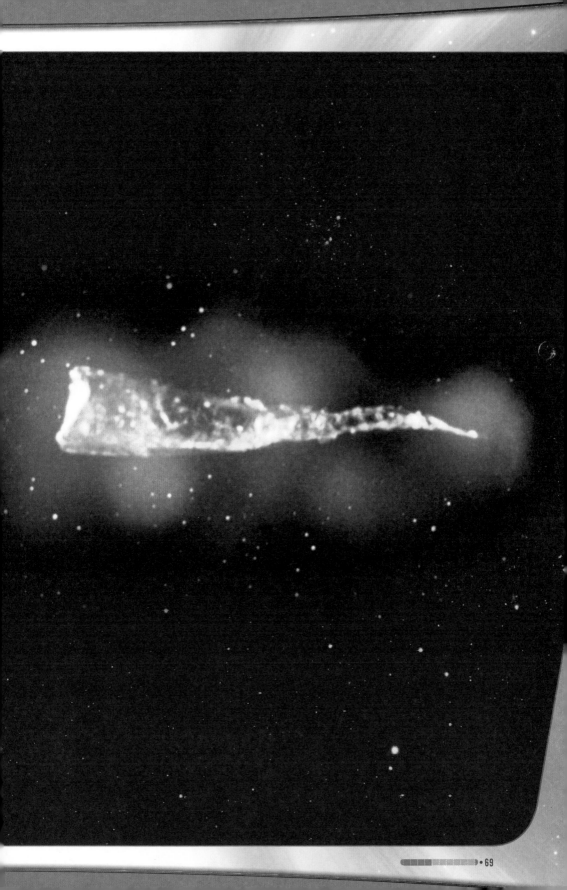

WHERE NOMAD HAS GONE BEFORE

On stardate 3541, heading towards the Malurian star system, the *Enterprise* came across an archaic interstellar probe of human design that had last been in contact with Earth more than 250 years previously. It quickly became obvious to us that the probe, which had fused somehow with an immensely powerful alien device, was responsible for the entire destruction of the Malurian civilization. More than four billion people had been killed. In an unexpected turn of events, Captain Kirk caught the probe, self-named Nomad, in a logical error, forcing it to self-destruct.

The *Enterprise* would later encounter an unusually similar situation in the form of the equally ancient *Voyager* space probe. Fortunately, that was resolved without the loss of billions of people.

As any engineer could tell you, an important concern when designing metal-based systems is to ensure sufficient temperature control. Metal is particularly prone to heat-related expansion. All materials are to a greater or less degree, but it can be quite noticeable in metallic constructions. When your components also include plastics, silicates and more advanced compounds, ensuring heat control becomes vital. Consider the very simple matter of a metal disk with a hole in the centre. As the disk is heated, does the expansion push at the hole, forcing it smaller, or pull it outwards, enlarging it?

STRANGE DREAMS

A number of statements are given below. For the purposes of this exercise, and only for the purposes of this exercise, you may assume that they are absolutely true in all particulars. Operating from that foundational assumption, you should be able to correctly answer the question that follows.

1. Thoughts are either logical inferences, or are ridiculous.
2. None of my thoughts about clouds are worth recording.
3. If a thought of mine is ridiculous, it invariably fails to be true.
4. Pass all my logical inferences to the captain.
5. I always dream about clouds.
6. Never pass a thought of mine to the captain if it is not worth recording.

Are my dreams true?

ANSWER ON PAGE 178

THE PIRATE

Let us hypothesize that a logically-minded space pirate desired to test the rational fitness of a group of minions. Having assembled them, he had them all stand in a single row, silent, eyes facing forward. They were not to attempt to communicate with each other in any way. Being a brutal disciplinarian, he made it clear to the group that any disobedience would be met with instant death. With the group thus obedient, the pirate moved along the back of the row, painting each person with either a black mark or a white mark.

Once each member of the group had received a mark, he took individuals out of the row, one by one. They were walked along the back of the row, so that they could observe every other member of the group, and then returned to their place in the line.

Then, he issued them a simple instruction – people with a white mark should advance a number of paces equal to the total number of white-marked individuals, whilst those with a black mark should advance one pace further, to differentiate themselves. Any who failed to place themselves appropriately would be executed on the spot as being unfit for duty.

How is this test to be passed?

MIRROR, MIRROR

On one memorable occasion, several of the *Enterprise's* officers, the Captain included, found themselves transported into a universe parallel to our own. It was distinguished from our own universe mainly by the heartless brutality of many of the indigenous inhabitants. Their version of the Federation was a savage empire, where promotion came through the murder of one's seniors.

For the sake of a simple logical exercise, let us suppose that in our prime universe, the Captain exclusively wore black socks, whilst in the mirror universe, he exclusively wore white socks. Further, let us say that when he transferred from our universe to the mirror one, his laundry wardrobe was partly transferred with him, so that his virtuous black socks were jumbled up with their evil, white twins.

I want to make it plain here that I do not ascribe moral agency to footwear, and that no such mixing occurred, to the best of my knowledge.

With that said, Kirk Prime now finds himself in a position where he urgently needs a pair of same-colored socks, in order to maintain the illusion of being in control, which odd socks would dispel. There are 16 white socks in his effects, and 13 black ones. He cannot be sure of the color of the socks that are going to be vended to him before they are delivered. He has time to make one request of this clothing supply. How few can he request and still ensure a pair of one color?

THE SIXTH DOOR

Having reached the sixth chamber of the maze, the candidate in the proto-*kolinahr* challenge had almost passed through half of the trials – the easier half. The final, 12th chamber was by far the toughest. In fact, whilst success rates in the labyrinth were quite variable year on year, on aggregate less than a third of novices managed to reason their way through to completion. Such impatience with imperfection indicates the regrettable state of Vulcan society during those troubled times.

The true *kolinahr* requires no such extremities, and there is little shame in withdrawing from it, or attempting it and failing. As I have mentioned before, monastic life is not suited to every person, even in a rational species such as ours.

Once again, the sixth chamber presented the novice with two doors, A and B, each bearing a sign. The working conditions of this chamber stated that if A was safe, then the sign on that door was true, whilst if B was safe, the sign was false. The sign on door A said, "It makes no difference which door you pick." The sign on door B said, "Room A is safe."

Which door should you pick?

It makes no difference which door you pick

Room A is safe

ANSWER ON PAGE 179

all in a row

On stardate 4153, the *Enterprise* was hijacked by an android, which had been masquerading as one of the regular new replacement crew. We were taken to an uncharted K-class planet, which we discovered was the new home of the human criminal Harcourt Mudd.

Whilst attempting to extricate ourselves from Mudd's android captors, several of the ship's senior officers were restrained, myself included. At one point, we were held in a line. Lieutenant Uhura was next to Ensign Chekov, but not to Captain Kirk. The Captain was not next to me. So who was I next to?

ANSWER ON PAGE 180

MUDD

The planet Mudd, immodestly so named by a human male of that name, was more correctly known as Galor IV. It was originally picked as an outpost of a now-extinct species, known as the Makers, who originated in another Galaxy. By the time the *Enterprise* was taken there, the only remaining inhabitants were androids, who had been despatched there to safeguard libraries of knowledge, and to research medical and engineering concerns. The planet later became a critically important Federation research post, and its android inhabitants both willing subjects and assistants in that research.

K-class planets such as Galor IV are broadly inhospitable, but can be made suitable for habitation through the use of pressurized domes and similar contrivances. There are some sports – specifically, individual fighter racing – that take place within the lower atmosphere of K-class locations. Galor IV has a particularly notorious track, and most zip-races there claim at least one life. A quick question then, for such a hostile location. If you are in a zip-race and overtake the person in second place, what position do you enter?

ANSWER ON PAGE 180

TEMPTATION

I recall a conversation taking place on Galor IV – at least, I recall the message of the participants' words, if not their precise phraseology.

UHURA: Half a million years in a young, healthy, pain-free body is very tempting.

CHEKOV: Yes, that would be very good.

KIRK: There could be consequences – a loss of humanity.

UHURA: Not if our own brains are physically moved over, surely?

MCCOY: It's not possible to know for sure without tests.

CHEKOV: The risk is better than aging to certain death in just a few decades.

UHURA: 999 out of 1,000 women would agree.

SCOTT: Men, too. So long as everything is functional.

CHEKOV: So then, it would be a good thing.

What logical error is Chekov demonstrating?

TROUBLE

On space station K-7, the crew of the *Enterprise* had their first encounter with *Polygeminus grex*, more commonly known as tribbles. Small, round, furry proto-mammals, the tribbles quickly gained the affection of the human crew. This was due in part to the cooing noise that the creatures admitted when petted, which had a noticeably relaxing effect on the human nervous system – an effect which has fortunately not yet been weaponized. Unfortunately, tribbles reproduce asexually and explosively, and their numbers quickly swelled to epidemic proportions.

In practice, a warm, well-fed *P. grex* will produce a litter of 10 once every 12 hours. But my purposes in this volume are to inculcate logical thought. So let me veer into scientific inaccuracy for a moment to say that if a tribble and a half produces a baby and a half in an hour and a half, how many and a half who spawn faster by half will produce a score – and a half – in seven hours and a half?

Game Show

Imagine, for a moment, that you are a participant on a game show. Such things are ubiquitous in the histories of all socially-complex species with driving forces that include greed and diminished empathy – those that go through a period involving widely broadcast popular media, anyhow. This phase has been suffered by most star-faring life in the Galaxy. Vulcan is relatively unique in that we had already adopted strong logical tenets before developing broadcast media, sparing our people a century or more of manipulation, indignity, physical insecurity, and pain.

Still. You are a game show contestant, and you very much want to win a prize one that is not a cabbage, or a heaped armful of tribbles. You have three boxes to select from. If you pick the correct one of the three, you win. Otherwise, you lose. You are not allowed to interact with the boxes in any way, and thus effectively must select one at random. Having done so, one of the two boxes you did not select is revealed to be an incorrect box, by the referee, who knows which is the correct one. Now that there are just two left, you are offered the chance to switch your selection to the other one.

Is it in your interests to do so?

LION

On stardate 4040, the *Enterprise* encountered a wrecked merchant ship near the planet 892-IV. Shortly after that, we intercepted television signals broadcasting the gladiatorial execution of the merchant ship's flight officer. On investigation, we discovered that the planet was a curious example of parallel development to Earth, having reached a technological level similar to that of 20th century on Earth whilst retaining an intact, powerful empire very similar to that of historical Rome. It is interesting that Romulan society also manifested many quasi-Roman traits. Hodgkin's Law of Parallel Development is a worthwhile area of study for those interested in such recurrent social phenomena.

During our time on 892-IV, Dr. McCoy and I were forced into gladiatorial contests ourselves. We survived without significant injury. In one of the matches following ours, several members of the heretical pacifist group The Children of the Son were set to fight a lion, placed at the far end of the 50-metre arena from them. The lion was wearing an unremovable metal collar welded to a ten-metre iron chain. Despite the Children's refusal to approach the beast however, it was soon amongst them.

How?

FaMILY MaTTERS

Family is an important consideration for most mammal-like species, particularly social ones. There is significant evolutionary advantage in a support structure that is likely to provide assistance to you, particularly when you are too small to feed, clothe and defend yourself. As species gain social complexity, understanding of social cues becomes increasingly vital, and again, being able to learn these intricacies whilst young, from a friendly adult, maximizes the chances of survival. The social contract typically suggests that in return for this assistance in early youth, the individual renders similar assistance when the parents are weakened by age.

It is no secret that my mother was human, but it would be a mistake to assume that Vulcans do not actually possess emotion. We do, as our history clearly shows. We just learn to set them aside as a bodily irrelevance, not unlike fingernail growth, or the digestive process. So in that sense, my human half has never been a weakness. A certain intuitive understanding of empathy is a social strength. My human great-grandmother had three daughters. Each of her daughters had one brother. So how many children were in the family in total?

GAV

The Tellarites are a truculent species. In addition to stubbornness and impatience, they make a deliberate sport out of provocation and argument. They are superlative engineers, however. There is often significant tension between Vulcans and Tellarites, as the Vulcan reliance on logic and emotional control is read as refusal to engage by the passionate Tellarites – one of the most offensive gestures to a species so driven by debate.

My father, Sarek, once claimed to have started a serious, life-long feud with a Tellarite by challenging him to a simple test of inductive logic. Taking a ceremonial cloth some two metres in length, Sarek challenged the Tellarite to place the cloth on the floor of the residential unit that they were in, so that when the pair of them stood on opposite ends of it, facing each other, they would be unable to touch. After a great period of time, during which he grew increasingly frustrated, the Tellarite accused Sarek of setting him an impossible challenge. My father then demonstrated how this could be accomplished. Can you see how it might be possible?

THE PARTY

Imagine that you and your partner are hosting a party for four other couples. The precise nature of this party is not important, so if you feel the need to do so, you may make the nature of this party anything that seems suitable to you. I have heard suggestions ranging from a 12-course Rigellian birthing banquet to an illegal underground boxing event. It is not important.

What is important is your discovery that, prior to the commencement of the party, each of nine other attendees had previously met a different amount of the other attendees. That is, none of the nine, including your partner, had previously met the same number of guests as one another. Since you yourself are included in the attendees, the others had therefore met from 1 to 9 of each other's number previously.

Obviously, acquaintance cuts both ways. If A has previously met B, then B has previously met A. Equally obviously, each person is well acquainted with their own partner.

How many of the attendees had you previously met before the party?

MILTON

The planet Zeta Bootis III was another that the Captain first encountered as a peaceful, pre-technological paradise. Unfortunately, on this occasion the Klingons had arrived a year before the *Enterprise*, and introduced significantly advanced weaponry to one faction. In the end, we gave the other faction similar weaponry, and left yet another formerly agrarian society shattered. Such is often the case when advanced civilization discovers simpler groups living on or near an exploitable resource.

Our initial purpose in approaching the planet was to perform some scientific research into the local plant life. So it is perhaps not unreasonable that the Captain and Dr. McCoy found themselves aiding the Captain's local contact, a man named Tyree, in the pursuit of a mugato, an ape-like creature with poisonous fangs. Before Captain Kirk joined the chase, Tyree was immediately behind the creature, with his wife Nona behind him, and Dr. McCoy behind her. Captain Kirk then joined them, and fell into place behind Nona. Tyree sped up, to flank the mugato on the left, and Nona also sped up, to flank the creature on the right. At this point, which participant was immediately behind the creature?

THE SEVENTH DOOR

Moving from the sixth chamber to the seventh, the novice attempting the ritual of logical mastery passed the half-way point of the test. In reflection of this symmetry, the chamber was closely similar to the previous one. It was not unknown for the bright but unwary to mistake the subtle differences here, an error which could prove significant.

The rules of this chamber were the same as those of the one before. There were two doors, A and B, and each bore a sign. Either door could open onto instant failure, or onto a way forwards. If room A was safe, the sign on its door was true. If room B was safe, the sign on its door was false. The two signs were also worded similarly to the ones in the previous chamber.

On door A, the sign read, "It makes a difference which door you pick." Sign B said, "Room A is safe."

Which door should you open?

It makes a difference which door you pick

Room A is safe

LIVING SPACE

On stardate 3211.7, Captain Kirk, Ensign Chekov and Lieutenant Uhura were preparing to beam down to Gamma II, in order to perform scheduled examinations on the unmanned astrogation beacon and communication relay there. As an uninhabited planetoid, Gamma II requires occasional oversight and upkeep from Federation crews. Prior to beaming down, the three were abducted by an advanced, long-range teleportation system. We eventually tracked them to the planet Triskelion in the M24 Alpha system.

The homeworld of a species who had long since transcended bodily concerns, Triskelion was ruled by a trio of remaining individuals, the Providers, disembodied brains who used their power in an unending series of violent gladiatorial games. Humanoids of all manners of species, collectively known as thralls and under technological domination, were made to fight each other while the Providers wagered amongst themselves on the outcome.

Thralls were bred on Triskelion as well as snatched, and the Providers had been entertaining themselves there for millennia. We discovered that the average time between generations of thralls was about 20 years. So test your intuition here, and rather than calculating the answer, take a guess: If you go back four centuries, how many direct ancestors would a typical thrall maximally have?

ANSWER ON PAGE 186

LIVING TIME

The Providers eventually agreed to wager the end of their enforced slavery of the people of Triskelion against the entire crew of the *Enterprise*. The deciding factor was Captain Kirk's performance in a three-against-one gladiatorial duel. Obviously the Captain won, or else I would not be writing this now. The Providers honored their wager, and allowed the thralls of Triskelion to form a free society, which they then assisted with a degree of guidance.

It is difficult to fault the Providers for becoming bored with their existences as disembodied brains, however lamentable it is that they decided on blood sports as a way of distraction. Time is a curious phenomenon, with an impact upon sentient individuals that often seems to be at direct odds with the dictates of the theory of special relativity. As a second examination of your intuitive facilities, take a guess at approximately how long a billion minutes is, in Earth years. Two months? Two years? 20 years? Once again, do not try to accurately calculate the answer.

aHaB

Argus X was a planet rich in tritanium ore that the *Enterprise* surveyed. Being 21.4 times harder than diamond, and with a melting point higher than current weapons technology can aspire to raise it to, tritanium is a valuable substance for several industries, including ship construction. Unfortunately, we also encountered a gaseous life-form that Captain Kirk had come across before, whilst still a Lieutenant. On that occasion, the entity killed half of the crew of the *U.S.S. Farragut*, the ship that then-Lieutenant Kirk was stationed on.

Captain Kirk admitted that he had delayed before firing on the creature when he first encountered it on the surface of Argus X some ten years earlier. Because of his delay, he had missed the creature. It then went on to ravage the *Farragut* and kill her captain, Stephen Garrovick – whose son, John Garrovick, was now an Ensign on the *Enterprise*, and badly injured by the entity himself.

The Captain felt a great deal of guilt about this situation, enough so that it led him to irrationally endanger the *Enterprise* and her crew. In doing so, what logical error of thought was he committing?

ANSWER ON PAGE 187

IMPROBABILITY

Imagine a new spaceship so advanced that it seems effectively miraculous to modern technology. Let us name it the *Heart of Gold*. The ship is built to withstand any level of stress. For its test flight, starting in Earth orbit, the ship is somehow pointed in a straight line out of the Galaxy, on a vector which will avoid all star systems in the Milky Way, and keep it away from any further galaxies.

The ship starts moving at impulse speed, but under ever-rising acceleration. After 30 seconds, it is moving twice its former speed. After 45 seconds, it is moving twice as fast again. It keeps accelerating in this manner, doubling its speed in half as long as the last time required.

Where will the ship be after one minute?

FIZZBIN

On Sigma Iotia II, the *Enterprise* witnessed a superlative demonstration of the damage that can be caused by violating the prime directive. The planet had been contacted a century before our visit by the *U.S.S. Horizon*, before the prime directive had been put in place. They left behind a paper and ink book entitled *Chicago Mobs of the Twenties*, which even then was over 170 years old. It is assumed this was accidental. Records are scarce, because the *Horizon* vanished shortly afterwards.

In the century that followed, the Iotians had rebuilt their entire society into a close facsimile of gangland Chicago as it was in 1920. In the end, the Captain decided to pretend that the Federation was an even larger criminal organization, and extort funds from the Iotians which could then be put to paying for a Federation overseer who would guide them towards a more stable society.

The Iotian love of card games reminds me of this logical challenge. Four cards are placed on a table. Each of them has a number on one side, and a colored patch on the other side. The four sides that you can see are 1, 2, white and black. It is suggested to you that – for these four cards specifically – if a number on a card is even, then the patch on the other side is white. What cards should you turn over to test this proposition?

HYDRATED

Gravity is an interesting phenomenon, one that we still have yet to completely understand, yet it is absolutely fundamental to the existence of all matter. Without it, nothing would exist; if it failed, nothing would survive. Now imagine, for a moment, that the universe is completely empty, except for two large spheres of liquid water. With nothing else to distract their movements, they would inevitably be attracted to each other. The gravity of the one would pull the other towards it, and vice versa, so that if they were of equal size, they would meet in the middle of the line linking their starting points.

Now, imagine something even less likely – that the universe consists of solely of pure, liquid water, except for two large bubbles of Earth air. You may assume that the universe is somehow endless.

How, if at all, would the bubbles be moved?

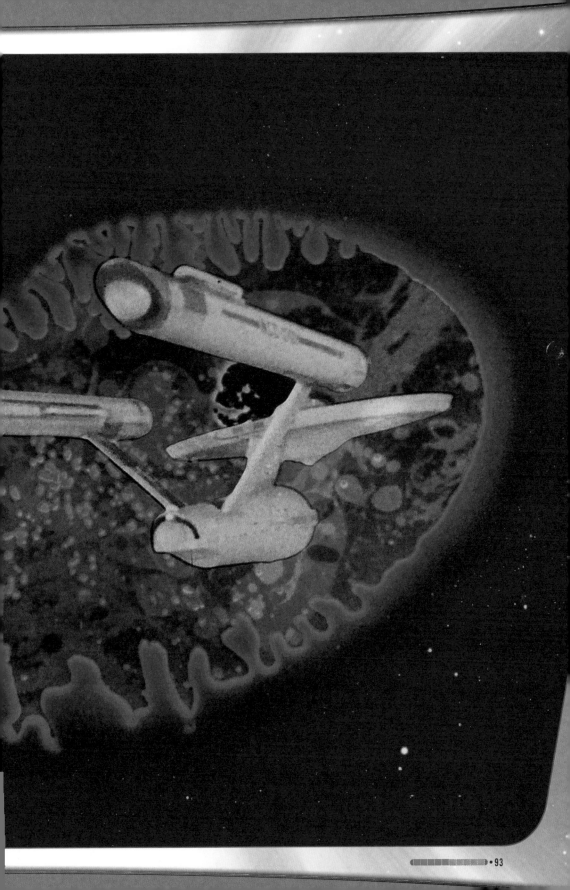

CONTINGENT

Whilst I was in the company of Jojo Krako, one of the dominant mob bosses of Sigma Iotia II, I overheard the man wrestling with a complicated problem involving several of his immediate underlings. Someone had clearly killed someone else, but getting to the root of the problem was taxing Krako to the limits.

Stripped of the assorted drama and counterdrama, the claims and arguments of the six men could be summarized as follows. I did not note their names.

A: F is telling the truth.
B: A is lying.
C: B is lying.
D: C is telling the truth.
E: A is telling the truth if D is telling the truth.
F: A is telling the truth if E is telling the truth.

Which, if any, of the six men are telling the truth?

POLYHEDRAL

On stardate 4657, the *Enterprise* was taken over by scouts from the Kelvan Empire, an advanced civilization in the Andromeda Galaxy – more than two and a half million light years away. Radiation levels in Andromeda were projected to make the Galaxy uninhabitable within a few thousands of years, so alternatives were being sought. The scouts had arrived in the Milky Way through the use of generation ships, taking centuries, but even such a feat was beyond Starfleet at the time. For the *Enterprise*, the journey would have taken millennia.

Despite their initial fixation on conquest, and the death of Yeoman Thompson, we were eventually able to persuade the Kelvan scouts to settle in the Milky Way and accept Federation assistance. Part of that assistance included sending automated vessels to the Kelvans, with offers to assist their entire species' relocation if they were prepared to be peaceful.

The question I have for you here is abstract, and related to the image I have chosen. In it, the Kelvan leader Rojan is demonstrating to the Captain that Lieutenant Shea and Yeoman Thompson have been reduced to simple matrices. Consider the natural two-digit numbers, from 10 to 99. Are there more with the first digit larger than the second, or more with the second digit larger than the first?

ROSTER

After the Kelvan Scout crisis, during which all but four members of the *Enterprise's* crew were transformed into small polyhedral masses, many on-ship routines were greatly confused. Extensive medical tests were required for a significant percentage of personnel, and sickbay staff became quite overworked.

One four-shift period was particularly affected by the chaos. Nurse Chapel was scheduled to work the first shift, but traded with Dr. M'Benga, who was originally down for the third shift, and Lieutenant Leslie switched with Dr. McCoy, who was originally down to work the fourth shift. Having remade these arrangements, Lieutenant Leslie had to change again because he was needed in Engineering, this time switching with Dr. M'Benga. Finally, Nurse Chapel became unwell, and her shift was changed with the following one, on Dr. McCoy's orders. Who worked which shift?

THE EIGHTH DOOR

The eighth chamber of the test that would become the *kolinahr* was the first to openly break from the established formula. It still had two doors, marked A and B, either of which could open onto either instant banishment, or progress onwards through the maze. There were also two signs, one belonging with each door. The rules of the room made it clear that if room A was safe, its sign was true, whilst if room B was safe, the sign was false.

This time however, the signs had been removed from the doors and placed in the centre of the floor, with no way to tell which door each belonged to. One of the signs said, "This room holds oblivion". The other said "Both rooms hold oblivion."

Which door should you select to progress?

This room holds oblivion

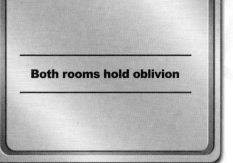

Both rooms hold oblivion

GaLILeo's ParaDox

It is a common layman's mistake to assume that rationality, logic and mathematics are all effectively interchangeable. The truth is that the three are significantly different. Logic is the process of induction which ensures that inferences are correct. Rationality is the process of basing thoughts on reason and factuality. Mathematics is the study of the measurements, properties and relationships between quantities. It is true that much of mathematics is both logical and rational, but true rationality in non-trivial situations requires conscious evaluation.

This is precisely why Vulcans train themselves in rationality, rather than simply handing all elements of our society over to computers. The real world is infinitely complex. Without consciousness, whether natural or artificial, there is little chance of simulated rationality mapping to rationality in the real world. The destruction of the *Enterprise's* sister-ship *Excalibur* – and the 400 lives aboard it – by the M-5 computer is a perfect example.

Consider this seemingly simple, logical, rational statement of mathematics: that there are more positive integers – 1, 2, 3, 4, etc – than there are whole square numbers: 1, 4, 9, 16, and so on. Obvious, yes? But it should be equally obvious that every number has a square number – 1->1, 2->4, 3->9, 4->16, and on endlessly. So there must be precisely as many positive integers as there are whole squares.

What is going on?

decrypt

Stardate 2144. The *Enterprise* received a transmission from a former Starfleet outpost once known to the Captain and myself as Cold Station 12, a biomedical Starfleet Medical unit, now believed to be abandoned. The message is a number repeated over and over again with no additional information embedded into the code.

The number was 8549176320.

Ensign Chekov, correctly remembering his Starfleet Academy communication training, believed the number to signify a primitive form of communication between Starship captains, known as Starfleet Ciphers, created when Starfleet was in its infancy. The ten-digit numeral would often go undetected by enemy warship signal scanners, but to human captains the number would signify a great deal more. The numbers were often a simple, but puzzling, encryption key device that once decoded, and resent to the original signal gateway location, would unlock a larger transmission message. These messages, in turn, would often then alert any nearby Starfleet starships of any impending enemy attacks on local bases, or the whereabouts of known Starfleet enemies.

Can you decipher the encryption code and decrypt what is unique about 8549176320?

O.K.

On stardate 4385, whilst attempting to contact a xenophobic alien race called the Melkotians, five of us found ourselves forced into a surreal recreation of a gun battle from old Earth history. As part of the illusion, each of the five of us was forced into the role of a historical individual, with his own very specific character and role in the unfolding violence, and equipped with a style of Colt .45 AAS pistol. Some notes about our characters now follow.

Tom drank moonshine – but was not the person who carried an "Artillery," who was wearing blue. The sarsaparilla drinker wore black, and did not carry a "Cavalry" or a "Civilian." One person was wearing red. Frank did not drink beer. Billy did not drink beer either, and didn't carry an "Artillery." Whiskey was the drink of the man who carried a "Storekeeper," who was not wearing cream. William, a different individual to Billy, carried a "Gunfighter." Ike, finally, was wearing gold, and did not carry a "Storekeeper."

Which of the five was drinking water?

PILLS

In the version of 19th century America that the Melkotians imposed on the *Enterprise* landing party, medicine was an extremely primitive thing. Healing was primarily based around pills of dubious efficiency, with less responsive issues requiring the use of extremely sharp knives to actually cut the sufferer open (and sometimes apart). Dr. McCoy was always appalled at the human medical technology of previous centuries.

Imagine that you have two different types of medical pill that you are required to take exactly one of each day. Accidentally, you remove one of the first type of pill, but two of the second type, and do not notice the error until the three are mixed together. The pills are visually indistinguishable, and cost a significant percentage of your income, so you are reluctant to be wasteful. At the same time however, taking a double-dose of one and a single dose of the other could prove catastrophic.

What options do you have to minimize waste and still ensure a correct dose?

ANSWER ON PAGE 195

PLATO'S DILEMMA

Sometimes, through no fault of our own, we find ourselves caught up in situations that are impossible to resolve. Life is full of little moments like this, particularly on Earth, and the ways that we find to address them are those things which truly define us as people. Captain Kirk, for example, famously approached his unwinnable Kobayashi-Maru scenario as a cadet in training by reprogramming the simulation so that his victory was straight-forward, rather than impossible. Indeed, much of his personality is founded on the principle that there is nothing that he cannot overcome. So far, he has been correct.

An archaic human thought experiment documents a similarly unfavorable situation. A philosopher by the name of Socrates approached a bridge over a deep gully that was owned and guarded by a warlord of some importance, named Plato. Socrates requested permission to use the bridge. Plato, thinking to gain some notoriety by crossing wits with a well-known philosopher, swore by the gods that if the next thing Socrates said was true, he would allow him to pass, whereas if it was false, he would throw him to his death in the rocky stream far below. Socrates replied that Plato was going to throw him to his death.

This left Plato in a hard situation. If Socrates's statement is accurate, Plato must let him pass. But if he lets Socrates pass, the statement is inaccurate, and the philosopher must be thrown into the ravine. But that would make Socrates's statement accurate...

What is Plato to do?

DOHLMAN

In the Tellun star system, the *Enterprise* was given a mission to facilitate a marriage of state between the rulers of the planets Troyius and Elas, traditional enemies. To that effect, we escorted a Troyian ambassador, Lord Petri, to Elas. Lord Petri's purpose was to attempt to prepare the Dohlman of Elas, a notably fierce woman named Elaan, for the realities of the significantly more genteel Troyian culture.

When the Troyian ambassador was found, barely alive, with an Elasian dagger in his back, we were confident that our would-be murderer was one of three – Elaan, her lieutenant Kryton, or one of his guards, Durock. As part of the investigation, we uncovered several verifiable facts. Only the three mentioned had possibly had access to Lord Petri at the time of the attack. Elaan was in possession of her dagger. Durock did nothing without an order from Kryton. Kryton was fond of the garrotte. Elaan's tears are highly narcotic. No Elasian would permit their weapon to be stolen. Durock was a highly trained killer.

Could we say confidently that Kryton was involved in the attack?

LIAR

Having been badly injured in an attack, Lord Petri of Troyius withdrew from the Elasian delegation on the *Enterprise* and would have nothing more to do with Elaan. This was probably for the best. Petri was a fussy, condescending person, used to politesse and circumlocution, whilst Elaan was direct and imperious, with no tolerance for pointless manners or deference. This cultural gulf was one of the many reasons why their planets had been at war for so long.

With the duties of 'civilizing' Elaan fallen to Captain Kirk, Petri was left at a loose end. I spent some time with him, taking the opportunity to learn a little more about the Troyian culture and technology. I gleaned little of use, but he did put an interesting question to me, a formulation of the paradox know to Earth philosophy as Epimenides's Paradox. "If I say to you 'this statement is a lie," Petri said, "then we have a problem, you and I. If I am telling the truth, then the statement is a lie, and cannot be truth; but if I'm lying, then the statement is true, and cannot be a lie. So the statement has to be simultaneously true and false."

Is he correct?

THE NINTH DOOR

After the alterations of the previous chamber, the candidate entering the ninth chamber of the proto-*kolinahr* discovered more alteration to the system – three doors offering possible progress, rather than two. If the first four rooms had eliminated the defective, and the second four rooms the incautious, then the final four were designed to remove the imperfect. Only the very best novices were permitted to advance.

In this room, the doors were labeled A, B and C, and each one had a sign, properly affixed to the correct door this time. The conditions of this particular chamber were such that exactly one of the doors led onwards through the maze, whilst the other two held instant unconsciousness. As for the signs, either none or one of them was true.

The sign on door A declared, "This room holds oblivion." Sign B said, "This room is the way through." Finally, sign C said, "Room B holds oblivion."

Which is the correct door to pick?

BRIDGE

Whilst attempting to deflect an asteroid from its collision path with a planet, the *Enterprise* suffered significant warp engine damage. Consequently, we had to spend almost 60 days under impulse power, traveling ahead of the asteroid back towards the planet's surface.

During that time, Dr. McCoy took to entertaining himself and certain other crew members by playing a traditional Earth card game named Bridge. In this game, the entire pack of cards is divided equally amongst four players. The dealer, who is the player responsible for giving out the cards, starts by presenting the top card – face down, of course – to the person immediately to his left, and then continuing clockwise around the quarter, giving one card each time until the entire pack is dealt.

On one occasion, in the mess, I overheard the doctor complaining that a particularly distracting annoyance had made him lose track of who should receive the next card. He concluded that it would be necessary to gather all the dealt cards up, and start the entire process again. He was of course incorrect.

The simplest option would be to have each player count the cards dealt to them so far. But even removing that as an option for some arbitrary reason, can you see how he could complete the deal whilst ensuring everyone got the cards they should have done?

new dawn

The planet from the story opposite held a hunter-gatherer civilization remarkably similar to the native American peoples of Earth. By examining an obelisk that demonstrated some extremely advanced technology, I was able to ascertain that this civilization's forebears had been deliberately transplanted from Earth centuries before by an alien civilization. Their records made it plain that they often saved endangered local cultures by moving them to distant planets specially terraformed to resemble their original homes in terms of atmosphere, flora and fauna. It seems near-certain that the Preservers are responsible for most of the pre-contact human civilizations scattered across the Galaxy, and the reason why so many of these resemble historical elements of human society.

It is common knowledge that the planet Earth is eight light-minutes from Sol, its star. The planet we were on had been given almost identical atmospheric and astronomical conditions to Earth. It too was eight light-minutes from its star. On two particular mornings each year, the sunrise on the planet occurs at precisely 6am local time. Let us say that tomorrow is one of those days. During the night, imagine that light from the star was somehow sped up to 1,000 times its normal speed. When would sunrise occur?

THE ROMULAN PROBLEM

On stardate 5027, Captain Kirk ordered the *Enterprise* to cross the Romulan Neutral Zone and violate Romulan space. The Captain had been acting erratically for some time, and appeared to have finally lost all pretense of reason. The Romulans swiftly apprehended the *Enterprise*. To prevent destruction, we agreed to allow them to transport the Captain and myself to the command vessel of the ships surrounding us. The Captain was swiftly locked up, whilst the Romulans discussed the peaceful surrender of the *Enterprise* with me as de-facto commander.

During my time on the Romulan flagship, I came to discover that a number of the crew had quite notable flaws of emotionality in their thinking. Let us imagine that I am somehow uncertain as to who suffered from what flaw. Examine the following statements: Either Gardun or Charvanek was filled with envy. Either Mikhol, Gardun or Tal was sadistic. Either Mikhol, Gardun or Charvanek was prone to violent savagery. Either Charvanek or Tal was overly credulous.

Which person suffered from which flaw?

THEA

My exposure to the Romulan crew and, in particular, their commander during the *Enterprise* incident was quite interesting in many ways. It is clear that they originally sprang from Vulcan stock, and it is suspected that they are the descendents of our people who rejected Surak's Time of Awakening. Romulan culture is highly militaristic, but like the compliant Vulcans, they too rejected wild aggression. They are more prone to expressing violence through subterfuge than through open hostility, and despite their xenophobia, are not averse to diplomatic relations.

So, let us imagine a Romulan ship commander named Thea. Under her rule, any wife who knows her husband to be unfaithful must execute him precisely at the midnight following her discovery. Any Romulan wife would be delighted to obey this order, and such an execution will be immediately broadcast to all wives aboard. However, whilst every wife knows about the extra-marital affairs of every husband other than her own, tradition forbids any person to inform a wife about her husband's infidelity.

Thea announces to the ship that at least one unfaithful husband has been discovered. How are the wives aboard the ship to comply with her rule?

FaLse anGeLs

Consider the following series of statements. Taken at face value, they are intrinsically meaningless, but for the purposes of this question – and only for the purposes of this question – you should assume that they are absolute and literal truth. Given this unlikely foundation, assess the statements in order to deduce an answer to the question.

1. No false angel is ever not well presented.
2. A spirit that cannot sing is flickering.
3. No spirit is well presented unless it sparkles.
4. All spirits, except false angels, are kind to children.
5. No blue spirits can sing.
6. A spirit that sparkles is never flickering.

Are blue spirits kind to children?

CHILDREN

A distress call led the *Enterprise* to the Federation outpost on Triacus in the Alpha Lyrae system. There we discovered the members of the Starnes Expedition dead by apparent suicide. Their children were unharmed however, and were conveyed to Starbase 4. The less said about that journey, the better.

The following pieces of information are all accurate.

Ray's surname is either Tsing Tao or O'Connell, and his favorite ice-cream is either banana or caramel. The child surnamed Starnes is either 9 or 12 years old. Don's favorite ice-cream is either vanilla or strawberry. The 11-year-old is either called Tommy or Steve, and surnamed either O'Connell or Starnes. The child who is 10 years old has either strawberry or banana as a favorite ice-cream. The child whose favorite ice-cream is chocolate is either 12 or 8. Mary's favorite ice-cream is either vanilla or banana, her surname is either O'Connell or Janowski, and she is either 10 or 9 years old. Steve's favorite ice-cream is either chocolate or banana, and he is either 11 or 10 years old. One of the children is surnamed Linden.

How old is Don?

BRAINS

On stardate 5431, my brain was stolen by a mysterious assailant. I realize how preposterous that sounds to say, but it remains the literal truth. After its successful recovery and reintegration, I put myself through a number of exercises to assess possible damage. One of these is performed as follows.

Obtain four tumblers or other simple drinking vessels, and a tray. Have an assistant blindfold you, and then place the tumblers on the tray so that some are upright, and some are upside-down. The challenge then is to ensure that all the tumblers are in the same orientation. This is accomplished through turns. During a turn, you are allowed to feel and, if you so desire reverse the orientation of, up to two tumblers. Once you have done so, the assistant will rotate the tray either 90, 180, 270, or 360 degrees, jostling it so that you are unable to tell how far it has been turned. Once all four glasses are in the same orientation, you will be informed.

Would you be able to get all the glasses to the same orientation, either upright or upside-down, within five turns?

Lionnais

Using an alien device known to the Eymorgs of Sigma Draconis VI as the Teacher, Dr. McCoy was temporarily powered with sufficient scientific and logical expertise to perform the complex surgery of reattaching my brain to the rest of my body. The knowledge did not stay with him for long, although it was my sincere hope that he would never be called upon to make use of such skills again.

In honor of his period of superior intellectual ability, please consider the following proposition. Many numbers have been described by mathematicians as interesting for various assorted reasons – two, for example, is the only even prime number; four is the only number which can be reached by both doubling and adding two to a given number. The list often seems endless. The human scientist Francois Le Lionnais claimed that the first uninteresting number was 39. If we accept this, then 39 becomes interesting by that very property, and thus has to void its claim. So we move on to the next uninteresting number, which then becomes the first uninteresting number, with the same problems. So can there ever be an uninteresting number?

ANSWER ON PAGE 202

STRIP

There are, in truth, some realities which the rational structure of the brain is ill-prepared to deal with. It would be illogical to claim otherwise. As I have intimated elsewhere, coping with these realities is the test that sets sentient and non-sentient intelligences apart. The sentient being may have the flexibility to adapt; the non-sentient will just shatter.

For a simple, practical example, take a strip of paper, turn one end through 180 degrees whilst keeping the other end in its original orientation, and then fasten the two ends together. How many sides has the resulting shape got? How many edges?

ANSWER ON PAGE 202

DEEP NOTHING

As just discussed, there are places, both practical and theoretical, where sense breaks down. Whilst transporting the Medusan ambassador Kollos, the *Enterprise* was temporarily bounced outside of galactic space and into the intergalactic void by passing warp factor 9.5.

On a similar basis, consider the possibility that $0 = 1$. The associative law of summation says that you may bracket simple sums however you wish without changing the result. So $(4+6)+8 = 4+(6+8)$. Now, consider that however many zeroes you add, they still give you zero, so $0 = 0 + 0 + 0 + 0 + 0 +...$ and on. $(1-1) = 0$, so you can replace each zero in your line with $(1-1)$, giving you $0 = (1-1) + (1-1) + (1-1) + (1-1) + (1-1) +...$ and on. But you can rearrange your brackets, by the associative law. Thus $0 = 1 + (-1+1) + (-1+1) + (-1+1) + (-1+1) + (-1+1) +...$ and, since $(-1+1) = 0$, then $0 = 1 + 0 + 0 + 0 + 0 + 0 +...$ which, since all those extra zeroes are irrelevant, gives you $0 = 1$. This is clearly untrue. What is wrong?

ANSWER ON PAGE 203

THE TENTH DOOR

Entering the tenth chamber of that which would become the *kolinahr*, the novice was again presented with three doors to choose from. As in the previous room, it was made known that one of the doors would lead on deeper into the maze, whilst the other two would provide only an instant banishment. Part of the purpose of the trial was for the novice to demonstrate clear thinking, free of emotion in extreme circumstances. The less encumbered by distraction the candidate was, the simpler they would find the problems facing them. In this sense, anxiety and fear were just as deadly as confidence or relief.

The rules of this chamber stated that of the three signs, that on the safe room was definitely true, whilst at least one of the other two signs was false. The sign on door A declared, "Room B holds oblivion." The sign on door B said, "This room holds oblivion." The sign on door C said, "Room A holds oblivion."

Which is the correct way forward?

Gems

On Minara II, the Captain, Dr. McCoy and myself encountered two members of a humanoid alien race who called themselves Vians. They were technologically advanced, and had been running tests on the scientists operating the Federation research station on the planet. The star Minara was in the process of exploding, and having examined – and killed – the human scientists, the Vians turned their attention to an empath woman from another planet in the system. Eventually, they decided that the woman's species was worth saving from the star's explosion, and that we all were to be allowed to live. Such tests are all too familiar to me from Vulcan's own history, as you know.

To my knowledge, the following question has never been a matter of species survival, but it would seem foolish to rule it out completely. You may wish to treat it appropriately.

If you choose one of the four answers A to D at random, what is the chance that it will indicate the probability of it being the correct answer to this question? A: 0%, B: 25%, C: 25%, D: 50%.

FEEDING TIME

For this question, I have for you a series of propositions. For the purposes of this question, I wish you to consider them to be exact and perfect truth. In reality, they are quite close to nonsense. Several human ensigns of my acquaintance have quite clearly demonstrated glimmerings of common sense from time to time, and I strongly suspect one or two lieutenants I know still indulge in playing hopscotch.

Nevertheless, treat the statements that follow as factual, and use this information to evaluate – and answer – the question at the end.

1. All humans – except ensigns – have at least some common sense.
2. No one who eats only candy can be anything but a fool.
3. Only hopscotch players know what real happiness is.
4. No fool has any common sense.
5. No lieutenant ever plays hopscotch.
6. No ensign is ignorant of what true happiness is.

Do lieutenants eat only candy?

RELIABILITY

Three weeks after the *Constitution*-class *U.S.S. Defiant* vanished in open space whilst investigating a distress call, the *Enterprise* was sent to search for her. We found her within territory claimed by the Tholian Alliance, but phasing in and out of our own dimension. Tholians are an insectoid species, known primarily for their xenophobia, precision, territoriality and silk. Their presence made retrieval of the *Defiant* impossible, and almost cost us Captain Kirk as well.

Whilst precision may seem a beneficial thing to a rational mind, its application needs to be sufficiently flexible to remain helpful. Consider the following hypothetical problem. Imagine that an inscrutable new alien race offers you the choice of three apparently indistinguishable ambassadors. Due to some quirk of psychology, the eldest of the three will answer your questions honestly, the youngest of the three will answer your questions dishonestly, and the middle one will answer your questions randomly. You are not informed which is which, nor can you tell, but you are instructed to choose an ambassador on the basis of a single yes or no question put to just one of the three. Once you have decided, you will be told which you have chosen.

The individual who is honest would be the best outcome, but the one who is reliably dishonest would be acceptable. Once you know that each answer is guaranteed false, it is simple to derive useful information. What question do you put to one of the three to ensure you recruit either the elder or the younger individual?

POCKETS

Towards the end of the *Enterprise's* encounter with the forces of the Tholian Alliance, they attempted to trap us in an energy net spun between two of their ships. Fortunately, we were able to break loose from their web before it was completed, leaving the instant that Captain Kirk was successfully reclaimed from the interspace pocket that he had been trapped in.

Even at the time, the incident brought to mind the following problem, which I recall from early training. There is a predator, and its prey. The prey is hiding in one of five spots, which are arranged in a straight line. Each spot is connected to those adjacent by safe passages. The predator is able to check one possible hiding spot at a time, after which the prey quickly moves to another spot. Call this exchange one 'turn'.

Assuming that the prey must move each turn, that there is no quick connection from first spot to last and that the predator is acting rationally, how quickly can the predator be certain of catching the prey?

ANSWER ON PAGE 207

DEFIANT

When we beamed aboard the *U.S.S. Defiant*, we found the entire crew dead from a very wide range of causes. Further investigation proved that they had killed each other (and themselves) indiscriminately, and when we retrieved the ship's log, the chief surgeon documented the spiraling violent insanity, but was at a loss to explain it. We finally discovered that a property of local space had a very powerful negative effect on the human mind.

The following data points provide details about five of the victims. Analysing this, can you say how the oldest of the five died?

The victim named Ward was older than the crewman. The victim killed by phaser fire was younger than the one who was stabbed, who was not the captain. Either Warfield was the captain and Malgarini was poisoned, or Ward was the captain, and Warfield was poisoned. Sussman, who was throttled, was five years older than the ensign, who was either Ward or Wong. The ensign was older than the lieutenant. Either Wong or Ward was 38, and was stabbed. Someone died from a snapped neck. There were victims aged 23, 28, 33 and 43.

yonada

On stardate 5476, the *Enterprise* was attacked by primitive nuclear missiles of a sort that had been out of date for two and a half centuries. Destroying them harmlessly, we followed their trajectory back to a generation ship disguised as a broadly spherical asteroid some 300 km in diameter. The ship was on a collision course with a densely-inhabited world, so we beamed down to it, and after some rather typical annoyances – Dr. McCoy was married and cured of a fatal disease, and Captain Kirk and I were sentenced to death at least once – we corrected its course.

Despite the technological advancement required to create a generation ship, the inhabitants of the *Yonada* were quite primitive. In conversation with one old man, he informed me of a time when he had made a lengthy journey through his world. One morning, he claimed, he had risen from bed, prepared for the day, gone outside his home, and then entered his vehicle. Then he'd travelled a distance equivalent to 150 kilometres in a straight line, through the wilds of the fake planet. He stopped and left his vehicle, re-entered his home, dined, and went to bed. He was absolutely firm that although he was 150 km from the location he'd been in the morning, it was the exact same bed in the exact same home, that his path had not curved in any manner, and that no teleportation or telepresence was involved. Can you explain the situation logically?

ANSWER ON PAGE 208

T'SENG

On one occasion during my childhood, I overheard three of my peers talking. The two boys were attempting to persuade the girl, T'seng, into revealing her birthday. She decided that they would have to earn that information. First of all, she gave them a list of ten possible dates. I have taken the liberty of transposing these to dates in the human calendar that are suitable to T'seng's original purposes, rather than to attempt to calculate which human dates the originals might have actually corresponded to. The latter path would rather destroy the girl's challenge, after all.

So, let us say that T'seng's possible candidate dates were April 7, April 16, May 15, May 16, May 19, June 17, June 18, July 14, July 16, August 14, August 15, August 17, September 9, September 12, October 11, October 13, October 14, or November 10. She then whispered the correct month to Soss and the correct date to Del, on the express condition that they promise not to reveal that information.

Soss then declared that whilst he couldn't tell the full date of T'seng's birthday, he was confident that Del could not either. Del replied that knowing that informed him of the full date. Soss replied that if that was the case, he too know the full date.

What was T'seng's birthday?

RAGE

Arriving at Beta XII-A near the Federation-Klingon border, the *Enterprise* sent down an away team to answer a distress call that she'd received from a colony of 100 civilians. According to the call, the colony had been under attack from a spaceship. Investigation revealed no remaining trace of a colony. Then Klingons arrived in a badly damaged ship, and attacked.

After some back and forth about who was capturing who, the Klingons were brought on board the *Enterprise*. At that point, an entity that had been on Beta XII-A started manipulating the minds of all on board to incite hatreds of any kind it could. The ship was nearly destroyed in the havoc this created, but we were able to ascertain the nature of the attack, and force the entity away by both humans and Klingons deliberately setting aside negative emotions in favor of positive ones. It is a rare thing to see a merry Klingon.

During the period of chaos, I was quite certain that I watched a group of three individuals start walking at very different speeds. One was ambling at 2 km/h, one walking at 5 km/h, and one nearly jogging at 7 km/h. After five minutes, the ambler turned to the jogger and whispered something in his ear, despite the fact that all three had started from the same location at the same time.

I quickly realized that my observation was correct. How?

THE
ELEVEN DOOR

Entering the penultimate chamber of the proto-*kolinahr*, the candidate was faced with another change in the overall system. Once again, there were three doors to choose from, but this time, one was certain to lead onwards, one led to instant ejection, and one led to temporary imprisonment for a period of hours, after which would follow unconsciousness and banishment. By this last twist of cruelty, the test aimed to threaten the novice with something worse than mere failure. If panic could not be suppressed, shame lay close by.

The conditions of the chamber stated that the sign on the door leading to safety was true, the sign on the door leading to banishment was false, and the sign on the pain door could be either true or false. The sign on room A said, "Room C holds pain." The sign on room B stated that "Room A holds imprisonment." The sign on room C read, "This room holds pain."

Which door would you pick?

A Room C holds imprisonment

B Room A holds oblivion

C This room holds imprisonment

PLAY

On Platonius, myself and several other senior members of the crew encountered a society of humanoids who claimed to have moved to the planet after spending time in the ancient Greek civilization on Earth. The very same individuals, so far as I could ascertain. They had journeyed to Earth from some other place as well, possessed of prodigious mental powers and extremely long lifespans.

During our semi-voluntary stay, the Platonians used powerful telekinetic and related powers to force us to perform for them in various manners, as if we were clowns, or traveling entertainers. Most illogical. One of the indignities was a little play, in which we were forced to pretend to be arguing over which of us had committed a crime. Consider the following situation. Five of us each make three statements, and one of each set of three is false. The other two are true. Assume nothing about our real interralationships and restrict your knowledge entirely to the statements given.

Nurse Chapel: "I'm innocent. Dr. McCoy is the guilty one. I've known Lieutenant Uhura for years now." Captain Kirk: "It certainly wasn't me. I've committed no crimes or sins. Lieutenant Commander Spock did it." Dr. McCoy: "I didn't do it. I know Lieutenant Uhura is innocent too. Nurse Chapel hates me." Lieutenant Uhura: "It was nothing to do with me. I've never seen Nurse Chapel before in my life. The Captain is right, Lieutenant Commander Spock is guilty." Lieutenant Commander Spock: "I am not guilty. Captain Kirk lied about me. Nurse Chapel is the guilty party." Which of us is guilty?

GRANDIOSITY

One of the entertainments indulged in by the Platonians was a large-scale form of a game not dissimilar to chess. This they played on a large section of tiled floor, rather than a board, using decorated marble pieces each weighing several hundred kilograms. Their telekinetic abilities made moving the pieces trivial, where a less-gifted species would find it extremely inconvenient to even drag one piece a short distance.

My hypothesis is that the game took place on the scale that it did in order to allow the Platonians to alleviate some deep sense of unworthiness, for in a culture made up of such a small number of members, displaying a game to a large audience is hardly a concern. There are few other practical advances to a two-player game needing an excess of 40 square metres in floor space.

A simple question, then. Two people played three games of chess. A win was worth one point, a draw worth half a point, and a loss worth zero points. They naturally started at zero points. At the end of three games, they both had two points. How?

ANSWER ON PAGE 212

speedy

The *Enterprise* answered a distress call on stardate 5710 that brought us to the planet Scalos, an uncharted world. The distress call described a volcanic catastrophe and a nation of almost a million people, including a city of over 100,000, but when we arrived there, we found the planet to be barren with just sparse vegetation and no discernable animal life. In fact, it transpired that the Scalosians, a near-human alien species, had been hyper-accelerated by contaminants thrown into the atmosphere by the eruptions. Unfortunately, their men had also been rendered sterile.

We encountered them 68 days after the disaster, a period which must have subjectively seemed like years, even centuries, for the Scalosians. They attempted to entrap the *Enterprise* and use its cryo-stored crew as breeding stock, but they were down to just five individuals by the time we arrived. Given their incredibly rapid frame of personal time, they must have died out shortly after we escaped – unless a remnant of the Preservers somehow rescued them.

In light of the five Scalosians, consider this problem. Five balls are placed into an opaque sack. Two of the balls are red, one is blue, one is gold and one is green. I select two of the balls entirely at random, examine my choice, and declare that one is red. What is the probability that the other is also red?

SCALOS

The fate that befell Scalos was unfortunate. Given the few remaining survivors we encountered, and the rate at which they lived their lives, there was little scope for the Federation to have assisted. Add in that the Scalosians were unaligned aliens who had resorted to effective piracy of human vessels, the political will to make an unusual effort would most likely have been lacking anyway.

Charitable interference is always a delicate issue, even when it is clear that the alternative is disaster. That is why the Prime Directive is so strictly adhered to. Perhaps a simple example will assist with this point. Let us suppose that you are in possession of a small fortune, which you intend to devote, in one intervention, to fighting world hunger. Let us further assume that, invested in the financial industry, your fortune will grow at a slightly higher rate than world hunger will, and that without your intervention, the nature of the world will not change.

You could intervene today, spare some from starvation. Tomorrow, you will have more money, and be able to help more people. But tomorrow, you will still be able to build your fortunes higher. Whatever day you pick to intervene, you will have more funds to help with on the following day. But if you never intervene, you never help anyone.

What is the logical course of action?

BLACK AND WHITE

On stardate 5730, the *Enterprise* discovered a stolen shuttlecraft that had been removed from Starbase 4. Its life support systems were failing, so we beamed the occupant aboard – an alien from a planet in the southern reaches of the Galaxy. The being, named Lokai, was humanoid and two-tone – black on his left side, and white on his right. Shortly afterwards, we encountered another of his species, Bele, whose coloration was reversed. Bele explained that black-right people were the rightful superiors of his race, and the black-lefts were fit only for enslavement.

Lokai told of a cruel game the black-rights played on black-lefts. Ten people would be lined up in single file, and have a black or white mark placed on the back of their heads. The order and selection were entirely random. The victims could see the marks of the people in front, but not their own or those behind, and to communicate meant death. Then, the rearmost person would be asked the color of their mark, and permitted to say just "Black" or "White." If they guessed correctly, they were set loose. If they were wrong, they would die. If they tried to say anything else, all ten were killed.

Logically, is there a way to maximize survival?

ANSWER ON PAGE 213

Last Pass

Whilst in negotiation with the government of the supposedly paradisiacal world Gideon, the Captain found himself spirited onto an identical replica of the *Enterprise*. It was deserted apart from himself and the Gideon ambassador's daughter, Odona. We eventually discovered that it was all a part of a highly illogical ploy to get the Captain's unwitting aid in dealing with Gideon's severe overpopulation problem.

Let us posit a slightly different situation, however. There are 100 passengers preparing to board a transport. They have each been assigned one of the 100 seats, and are queued to board in seat order, first to last. However, the first person in line is irrational, and decides to pick a seat at random to sit in. Each following passenger is rational, and will sit in their correct seat if available, or a random seat if it is not available.

How likely is it that the last passenger is able to take their proper, last seat?

THE TWELFTH DOOR

The twelfth and final chamber of the proto-*kolinahr* logic trial was substantially larger than any that had gone before. It was by far the most perilous in the entire maze, and possessed of significantly greater complexity. The rules that governed it stated that one of the rooms was safe, and the sign upon its door was true. Of the other rooms, some held gas that caused unconsciousness, and the signs on those doors were false, and some led to hours of imprisonment before banishment, with the signs on those being either true or false.

If a sign linked two or more statements with 'or', then it was true if just one of them was true, whilst a sign linking multiple statements with 'and' was true only if all were true. If statements were linked with 'and/or', then the sign was false only if all of the statements were false.

An occasional response, at this point, from the very best, was to protest that there was no definite solution. Having so protested, the novice would be told that this was true – but if he or she knew whether room H led to imprisonment or not, the chamber would be solvable.

Which is the correct door?

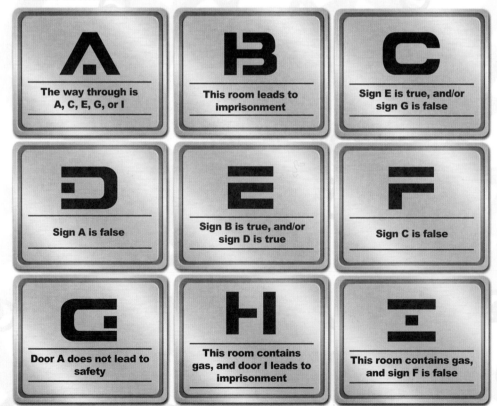

A — The way through is A, C, E, G, or I

B — This room leads to imprisonment

C — Sign E is true, and/or sign G is false

D — Sign A is false

E — Sign B is true, and/or sign D is true

F — Sign C is false

G — Door A does not lead to safety

H — This room contains gas, and door I leads to imprisonment

I — This room contains gas, and sign F is false

MEMORY ALPHA

Memory Alpha was the first of the Federation's library outposts, an open collection of knowledge about the Federation and the Galaxy as a whole. It was based on a planetoid in the Teneebia sector, within an otherwise unimportant system that came to be known as the Memory Alpha System. At the time of our visit on stardate 5725, during the objective Earth year 2269, it was the only such outpost, but we discovered that an aggressive alien presence had caused massive damage and total depopulation. Consequently, a back-up facility named Memory Prime was later created.

Memory Alpha contained a huge range of charts and maps. Imagine for a moment that the planetoid holding it was perfectly spherical to within any tolerance you can measure. This is, of course, effectively impossible, but set that aside for now. If you were to select three entirely random points on the planetoid's surface, what is the chance that all three would lie within one hemisphere? You may assume that the dividing line between hemispheres is vanishingly small.

ANSWER ON PAGE 215

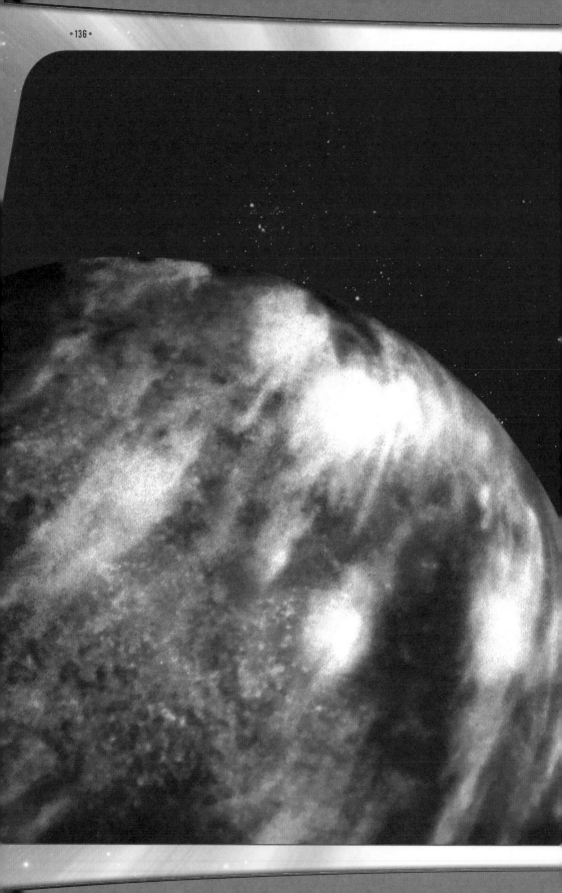

ardana

The *Enterprise* came to the planet Ardana in search of an extremely rare and somewhat toxic mineral called zenite. This was urgently needed to help the people of the planet Merak II produce medicine to fight off a botanical epidemic. Arriving there, we discovered that the Ardanans were struggling against an uprising of their mining caste, whom the wider society treated as mindless savages. Captain Kirk was forced to take an unusually interfering standpoint, assisting the miners, in order to secure the vital supplies.

Ignoring physical and physiological difficulties, it seems logical to say that if you are at the north pole of a planet, it is impossible to look north. Likewise, if you are at the south pole of a planet, it is impossible to look south. Obviously, these are local rather than interstellar directions we are discussing, and set aside such sophistry as "looking down at the ground."

Having established these loci of impossibility, where would you have to be to be able to look towards either north or south, but neither west nor east?

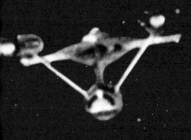

ANSWER ON PAGE 216

LITTLE MINDS

On stardate 5832, the *Enterprise* apprehended a stolen spaceship, the *Aurora*. The thieves attempted to flee, and overloaded the craft. Shortly before its destruction, we beamed the six occupants aboard. On their arrival, we discovered that the group were seeking the mythical planet paradise of Eden. Unfortunately, one was the son of an important ambassador, and so we were ordered to treat them delicately.

The spiritual leader of the group, Dr. Sevrin, told us a number of wild stories, but also gave us some information regarding actual responsibility for the theft of the *Aurora*. He said that only Adam, Mavig or Tongo might have stolen it. If Adam was the thief, he had exactly one accomplice. Furthermore, if two people were guilty, Adam was definitely one of them. He also said that if Mavig was innocent, then Tongo was as well, and that the obverse also held true.

What conclusion can be drawn from this?

FRICTION

The *Enterprise* discovered an ancient, reclusive former resident of Earth on the planet Holberg 917G. Flint, as he was calling himself, had been born some time shortly before 3,800 BC in the human calendar, in the Mesopotamian civilization. In the year 2239 AD, thoroughly sick of humanity's ongoing incivility, he used his then-colossal wealth to purchase Holberg 917G outright. He retired there alone, and devoted his time to the construction of a series of idealized female androids, attempting to create a wife whom he would not outlive. Our visit was not helpful to him, on balance.

Setting Holberg and its inhabitant aside, imagine a very large, perfectly frictionless table exists somewhere on the surface of the planet Earth. You have been placed at the centre, naked and prone, and you are unable to reach out to contact any of the edges. You are unable to pull or push yourself, and you lack the perfect coordination required to get to your feet on such a surface. How might you go about getting off the table, without outside help?

PARANOIDS

Seeking to investigate the nature of good and evil as understood by humanoid species, the Excalbians, a silicon-based life form, invited Captain Kirk and myself to land on their planet. They did this through a close recreation of Abraham Lincoln, a respected figure from Earth's history. We then discovered that they'd also recreated the Vulcan philosopher Surak, whose work started the Time of Awakening – and a group of equally eminent dictators and murderers. Their intent was to test 'good' versus 'evil'. The Captain and I survived, although I wonder how much the Excalbians learned.

Seizing on the historical theme, let us imagine that an early human historian has unearthed a valuable artefact, and wishes to transport it to a colleague. He does not trust his courier. He is able to seal the box with a strong padlock, but refuses to give any key to the courier, at any time. Without a key, his colleague will be unable to open his lock, but unless he has added a padlock, he fears to send the box. His fears are unfounded – the courier is utterly incurious regarding the box – but nothing will convince either historian of this. Is there an option that can convey the artefact to the colleague without either of the historians having to leave their work and make a journey?

ZARABETH

Having travelled to the planet Sarpeidon to warn the inhabitants that their star was about to go supernova, the Captain, Dr. McCoy and myself discovered it was nearly uninhabited. It turned out that the residents had fled to a range of times in the planet's past. Just one individual, a librarian named Atoz, still remained. For a brief period, the Doctor and I were transported back into a barbarian ice-age, whilst the Captain ended up in a time analogous to Earth's 17th century. Going unprepared through the time portal was not conducive to sanity or health, and we had to return before we were killed by the effect, but there was no harm done in the end.

Sometimes, forces of attraction are larger than resistance can overcome. Hypothetically, imagine that the only material body in the universe is a large, hollow sphere of rock 100 km in radius, and three metres thick. If a tennis ball were then to be introduced into the space inside the sphere, at rest and at a randomly determined point, what would happen to it? Would the shell's gravity pull it towards the middle, or to the nearest edge, or to some other point entirely?

FINALE

Answering a distress call from an archaeological team on Camus II, we discovered an old friend of the Captain's, Dr. Janice Lester. She was very ill. Unknown to the rest of the crew however, she managed to use an ancient device belonging to the long-extinct natives to switch bodies with the Captain. Then, pretending to be James Kirk, she ordered the tranquilization of the body of Janice Lester, and proceeded to take control of the ship and crew. Ultimately, she and her accomplice took too long trying to kill the Captain in the body of Janice Lester, and the transfer reversed, shattering Lester's mind. Even before then, increasing errors of judgement and logic made it plain that something was wrong with the apparent Captain Kirk.

On the subject of errors of logic, I have one last problem for you. How many of the following ten statements are true, and how many false?

At least one of these statements is false.
At least two of these statements are false.
At least three of these statements are false.
At least four of these statements are false.
At least five of these statements are false.
At least six of these statements are false.
At least seven of these statements are false.
At least eight of these statements are false.
At least nine of these statements are false.
All ten of these statements are false.

ANSWER ON PAGE 220

answers

CHESS

False. From the two statements given, I am better than James, who is better than Mongomery, who is better than Leonard; and Nyota is better than Montgomery, but we have no information regarding her comparison to James or I. Leonard is clearly the worst out of all of us.

FUZZY LOGIC

Wishful thinking, or the appeal to consequence. This is one of the most common forms of human irrationality. Faced with an overwhelming desire that fact X be true, you decide, contrary to any logic or deduction, that X must therefore be true. It is perfectly understandable, given the power that your emotions hold over you, but none the less damaging.

BALOK

This is a prime example of argument by slogan, the logical error of believing style over the lack of substance. Balok states, in a persuasive manner, that the *Enterprise* will be destroyed; therefore, Lieutenant Bailey believes, the *Enterprise* actually will be destroyed. But persuasive words are not a logical argument. They are just words. Humans are very susceptible to this sort of manipulation. Always look for the evidence backing up glib assertions.

TRACTOR

Since the two were then on the same vessel, they logically must have been the same distance from the *Fesarius*. Do not allow irrelevant detail to confuse you.

THE FIRST DOOR

Door B offers progress. B asserts that one door leads to safety, the other to oblivion. A makes the same assertion, but is more specific about which is which. Precisely one of the two must be true, but A cannot be true without also making B true. Thus A must be false. Since A says that B leads to oblivion, and is false, then B must be the way through.

WARPED

No. Warp coils are exposed to radiation, and being unsafe makes them ugly.

HONESTY

Just one is positive. It is the only way to guarantee that any possible pair has at least one negative.

DIVISION

After 50 such operations, your stack will be a little less then ten Astronomical Units high – where one Astronomical Unit is the distance between the planet Earth and its sun, around 150 million kilometres.

INTUITION

Wrong. There are three coins, and *you* may not know which coin is which, but they are still three separate items. Each can land showing one of two faces, so there are 2*2*2 = 8 different possibilities. These possibilities are MMM, MMP, MPM, MPP, PMM, PMP, PPM and PPP. Only two of these eight possibilities show all three faces the same, MMM and PPP. Therefore the chance of all three coins landing showing the same face is 2/8, or 25%. If you are in doubt regarding this result, I encourage you to try it with a reasonably lengthy series of tosses, and count the results.

POLYWATER

12. If, at the end state, there are twice as many uninfected as infected, then two-thirds of the group is uninfected. The difference between one-half and two-thirds is 2 people; it is also, arithmetically, one-sixth of the group. Since one-sixth is two, the whole group must be 12 people.

THE
SECOND DOOR

Door B. If the two signs are both false, then B requires that A be the path through, whilst A requires that neither room be safe. Thus the signs are both true, and A contains gas, whilst B is the way through.

INSTRUMENTAL

None of the four statements is supported by the three propositions. We know nothing about the furniture owned by musicians. We are told of hand-held and keyboard string instruments, but not that they are the only possibilities. We are told nothing about percussion instruments. Finally, we are not told that keyboards have to be stringed instruments.

ROMULANS

The operator was punished for falling asleep on night duty. Personally, I suspect the story to be apocryphal rather than based in any fact.

THE BIGOT

The fallacy of damning the source, argument ad hominem. In abstract form, an ad hominem attack says that because X is somehow bad, whatever X is saying is also bad by association. This is, of course, nonsense. Logically, assertions should be weighed on their own merits, rather than those of the person presenting them. Ad hominem attacks are frequently used as deliberate manipulation in human public debates in order to downplay the importance of a fact that disagrees with the conclusions you wish to arrive at. The truth is that such interjections are irrelevant – logical deduction must be independent of any bigotry.

2=1

The mistake lies in simplifying the factored equation by dividing both sides by (x-y). As x = y, then (x-y) = 0. Anything divided by 0 becomes infinite. So what we are actually showing is that an infinite number of 1s is equal to an infinite number of 2s, which is effectively accurate.

OUBLIETTE

He does not need to tunnel around the walls to escape. He only needs to excavate a mound of earth high enough to bring him within reach of the opening.

QUINN'S PARADOX

As the pain slowly builds, there will come a point – let's call it x – where you think that the financial reward is not worth any noticeably greater pain. You should then stop after the following activation, that is, before $x+2$. Even though you would be unable to tell the difference between $x+1$ and $x+2$, the difference between x and $x+2$ would be noticeable. Having endured $x+1$, it may be tempting to continue, but then you are falling back into irrationality, like the mythic frog boiling in a pot.

ALL IN A ROW

As previously established, he was called Brian. Beware of false sequences in logical deduction.

THE CHAIR LEG

He threw it straight up. Try not to allow vague word choice blind you to rational necessity.

SCIENCE

It's 1 in 5, or 20%. The probabilities that the three scientists report are not related. The fact that they all claim a 1 in 5 chance of error does not mean that the actual probability of error is 1/125. It just means that they agree that it's 1/5. If one is wrong, all are wrong; if one is right, all are right. Probabilities only affect each other when they are independent.

GALILEO

We would have had to travel infinitely fast. A unit distance at 15,000 km takes as long to travel as twice that distance would do at 30,000 km. In other words, the distance there at speed X takes as long as the distance there and back at speed 2X.

JURISDICTION

It may be unsatisfying, but the only answer – logical or otherwise – is that the possible range of circumstances are too complex to allow for a logical general rule. These issues have to be decided on a case by case basis.

THE THIRD DOOR

Either door. If B is false, then room A contains gas, which would mean that door A's either-or was true. Since both signs have to possess the same truth or falsity, that is impossible. So the two signs have to be true. Sign B makes it clear that room A is the way forward. For sign A to be true, then room A cannot contain gas, room B has to be safe as well.

CHAINS

With no information to tell you otherwise, the only logical assumption is that the Captain would still be in command if I was killed. The direct line of authority ran Captain Kirk – myself – Lieutenant Commander Scott – Lieutenant Commander Giotto – Lieutenant Sulu – Lieutenant Uhura.

BLACKMAIL

The crime comes in the conjunction of the two acts, not their individual element. Likewise, being in public is not a criminal act, and neither is having sexual intercourse, but doing both simultaneously remains a public order offence.

NIGHT SHIFT

We know that Hadley = 5, that Hansen = 8, and that Kyle = 15. DePaul > 8, but DePaul + 5 < 15. Therefore DePaul worked nine continual nights.

THE FOURTH DOOR

Since the signs are the same, they are both either true or both either false. If they are true, then room A is the way through, and room B contains gas. This contradicts what the signs say, so they have to be false. Since the sign on Room B is false, it is safe to enter.

CRATES

Take a ball from the crate labelled as the mixture. It is mislabelled, so the color of the ball indicates all of that crate's contents, and you can place that label on it. Then, since all three labels are wrong, the third crate's label can go on the crate you just removed the label from, to be replaced with the mixture's label.

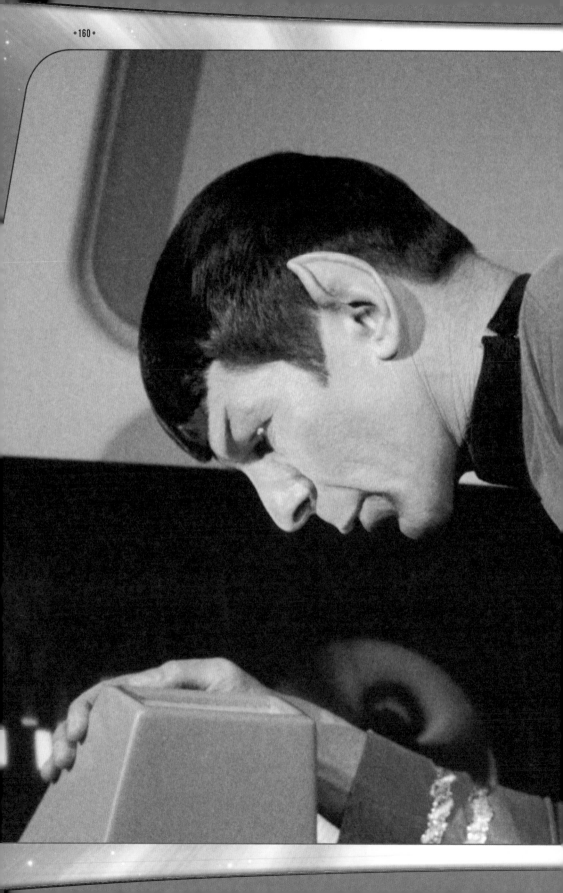

TIME

Light one fuse at both ends, and the other at just one end. When the first fuse is completely burnt, 30 minutes have elapsed, and 30 minutes of burn time remain on the second fuse. At that point, light the second end of the remaining fuse. It will then be completely burnt in precisely 15 more minutes.

LIGHT

Turn on switch A, and leave it on for fifteen minutes or so. Then turn it off, turn on switch B, and proceed briskly to the lamp. If the lamp is lit, switch B is the correct one. If the lamp is off, feel the bulb. If the bulb is hot, switch A is the control. If the bulb is cold, switch C powers the lamp.

BI-PLANETARY

The train traveling against the planet's spin will wear its wheels out first. Its velocity cancels out the centrifugal forces arising from the planet's rotation, so the train's entire weight bears on its wheels. The other train benefits from centrifugal forces from both its own rotation and the planet's rotation, reducing its effective weight.

GORN

No. The Gorn was to the south-west of the Captain.

Lazarus

The error is false dichotomy. Rhetoric of this sort is deliberately manipulative and dishonest. The supposed argument states that either X or Y is true, and Y is unthinkable, thus X, the desired outcome has to be true. Logically speaking, this is nonsense. The vast majority of the time, there are plenty of instances where neither X nor Y need be true. By reducing choices down to the desired result and an unthinkable alternative, the manipulator attempts to force others to accept their position.

Stardating

Only statement 2 can be logically derived from the given facts.

context

Divide the 20 disks into two groups of ten howsoever you choose. Ignore one of the groups completely. Flip each disk in the other group once. However, the disks are already arranged in a 50/50 split with marked/unmarked sides showing, however many marked-side-up disks you have in the first group, you will have that many unmarked disks in the second group. Flipping the second group will convert unmarked sides to marked sides, and vice versa.

.

DETERRENCE

This is one situation where rationality is perhaps less effective than irrationality. The rationalist, being sane, can never effectively employ a devastating deterrent against an enemy who understands the rationalist's mind. Bluff remains perfectly possible, of course. It is probably the only way a rationalist could genuinely attempt to deter. But even abstracting the decision to an automatic retaliatory system remains illogical, for what sane being would wish to harm vast numbers of the innocent purely because of a drop in status? Thus the irrational will often emerge the victor against the rational – in the short term. In the longer term, rational strategies, being much less self-destructive, will prevail. However, perhaps you begin to see why I served willingly under Captain Kirk

KHAN

Singh had slipped into the biased sample fallacy. Possibly the most common way of manipulating statistical evidence, this error occurs when one assumes that a specifically selected subset of people represent all people. In this instance, Singh's poll shows only that his followers think as he does – which is not a surprise, given that they are his followers. Representative samples have to be selected randomly in order to be effective as a statistical measure.

PARADISE

Jeannie, who had once had a knife scar, was a textile specialist, and now worked as a farmer. Leila, who'd had a bad knee, was a botanical specialist, and worked as a teacher. Elias, who'd had prenumonia-scarred lungs, specialized in agriculture, and served as the colony's mayor. Michael, who'd once had a badly-broken nose, was a medical specialist, and worked as a tiller. Grant, who used to be missing a finger, specialized in animal husbandry, and worked as a crafter.

BOOKWORM

Ten centimeters. When the spine of a book faces you, the front cover is on the right hand side. So the journey is from the rear cover of book two, to the front cover of book two.

CAUTION

They both faced Rynar.

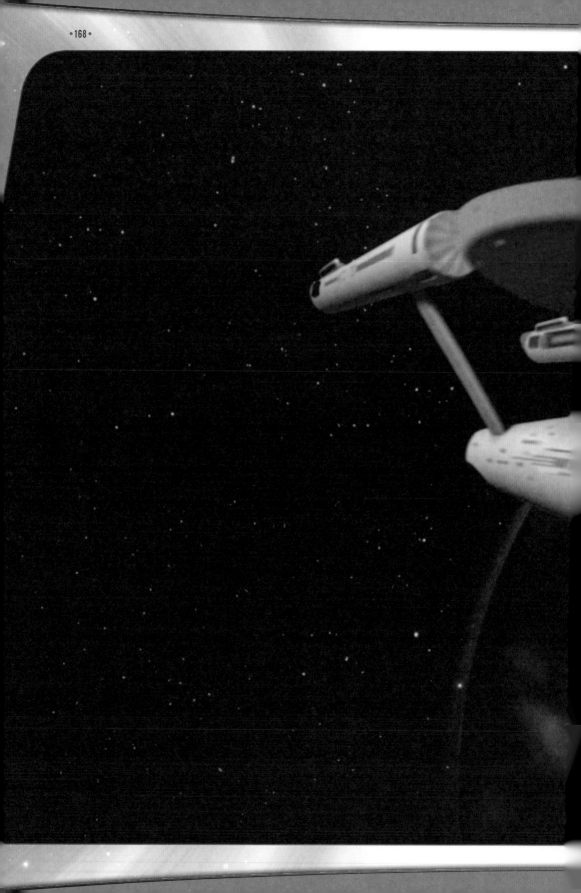

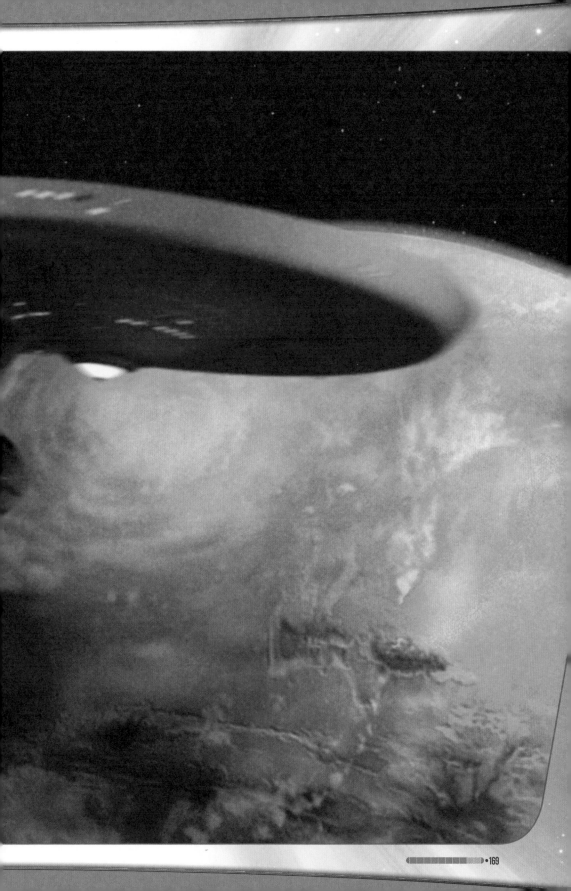

HERACLITUS'S PARADOX

The paradox arises, as hinted at it the early part of the question, because of the limitations of language. If you take the word 'river' to mean "Exactly this body of water in its current arrangement," then the river is eternally changing, a different thing from moment to moment. If, however, you take the word to mean "whatever water is currently flowing past this location," then the river is ever static, and never changes. So, rationally, the first step would be to precisely define the words 'river' and 'same'. Once those things are absolute, the paradox will dissolve into statements which are either correct or incorrect.

PETER

Such a person could – but does not have to be – your father.

THE FIFTH DOOR

Assume the case that room A contains gas. If so, then sign A has to be lying (by the room's rules), and B is clearly lying (by its content). But if sign B is lying, then room B must be the way through, and that would make sign A true. This is contradictory, which means room A cannot contain gas. Thus A is the way through. Signs A and B are both true, room A is the way through, and room B contains gas.

nine Lives

The incident occurred during daytime, so the cat was clearly visible. It is easy to be so swamped by seemingly congruent detail that one loses track of the absence of core critical data. When you are presented with a lot of information in agreement, always ask yourself what information might be being withheld.

TRINITY

The person in gold cannot be called Gold, and is not called Black, so must be called Green. The person called Black cannot be wearing black, and is not wearing gold, so must be wearing green. That leaves the person wearing black, who must be called Gold.

BURNING BRIDGES

The fallacy of argument from ignorance, which at its most basic, states that since A cannot prove argument X is false, then X must be true. This is, of course, utter nonsense. The burden of proof for any theorem, from the self-evident to the impossible, lies with the evidence for that theorem. The rational mind would never accept a proposition which used "falsify it yourself" as its only evidence in its favor. For example, consider the theory that you and your reality are not real, but an illusion in which you are compelled to ever believe yourself real and capable of thought. Can you prove otherwise? Does that make the theory true?

HaTS

It is blue. If the person at the end could see two red hats, it would be obvious that only blue hats remain. So the front two hats must include at least one blue hat. The person in the middle reasons this out. If your hat were red, the person in the middle would see this and know that their own has to be blue. As they do not, they must have seen that your hat was blue.

THE BOWman

Put the hat on the end of the arrow. When it is fired, the arrow will go through the hat. The Captain's tale said nothing about the arrow hitting the distant target.

apollo

This is an example of the straw man fallacy. Put simply, this is a rhetorical tool used to discredit an opposing argument through gross misrepresentation. Person A states X. Person B claims that person A is actually stating an unthinkable caricature of X, and thus that X is false. Most often, the Straw Man fallacy is a deliberate attempt to manipulate an audience.

Tournament

Every competitor save the overall victor must lose once. Therefore there are 127 matches.

LLAP

None. A handshake requires two willing participants, and there is no pair of attendees which does not have one shorter member.

REDJAC

Rigel IV. In sequential order, the hosts are: an Earth surgeon named Jack, with black hair, who wielded a scalpel; a Mars Colonies miner named Penny, with yellow hair, who used a pickaxe; a Deneb II dancer named Kesla with brown hair, who used a garrotte; a Rigel II hunter named Beratis, with blue hair, who used a hatchet; and an Argelius II administrator named Hengist, who was bald, and used a dagger.

SYSTEM SHOCK

Since there are no deciles when the two systems were malfunctioning simultaneously, to find the answer, maximize the number of deciles where no system was malfunctioning, whilst still allowing enough time for all the malfunctions. Two deciles of full normal function reduce your 6+7 functional occasions for the individual systems to 4+5, so add 4 deciles for when the warp engines malfunctioned, and 5 deciles when the transporters were broken, for a total of 11 deciles, or 1.1 days.

WHERE NOMAD HAS GONE BEFORE

The hole expands, as the piece of metal keeps the same proportions.

STRANGE DREAMS

No. My dreams of clouds are ridiculous.

THE PIRATE

The solution is simple. Assume you yourself have a white mark. Sum up all the white marks you can see, then add one for yourself. If you are correct, then advancing that number of paces will put you in the correct position for a white-marked individual. If you are wrong, and bear a black mark, you will be one pace in front of the white-marked people, and thus again in the correct position.

MIRROR, MIRROR

Three will suffice, as with two possibilities, three guarantees a match. If he wanted to be certain of two *white* socks, he would need to request 15.

THE SIXTH DOOR

If sign A is true, then its accuracy makes it the way through, and by extension, door B must be the way through. If sign A is false, then the rooms have to be different, and since sign A is lying, it holds gas, and room B must be the way through. So either way, door B is safe. Since door B is safe, sign B must be a lie, thus room A is not safe. Both signs are false. Room A holds only gas, and room B is the way forward.

ALL IN A ROW

Uhura. Kirk is not next to Uhura or myself, so he must be at one end of the line of four, with Chekov next to him. We know Uhura is also adjacent to Chekov, so she's next. That just leaves me, at the other end of the chain from Kirk.

MUDD

Second, clearly. You need to overtake the leader to enter first place.

TeMPTaTION

By assuming that an overwhelming show of agreement means that something has to be true, Chekov is commiting the fallacy of groupthink, often referred to as the appeal to common belief. It is an error, nothing more. Truth is not a democracy. Even if the entire population of Earth had once believed that the planet was a flat plane rather than a globe, that would not have made them correct.

TROUBLe

One tribble. If 1.5 T produce 1.5 more in 1.5 hours, then 1 T produces 1 more in 1.5h. Then, a tribble that spawns faster by half by producing 1.5 more in 1.5h, or 1 per hour. So, in 7 + 7/2 = 10.5 hours, 1 faster tribble will produce 20/2 + 0.5 = 10.5 tribbles. If you got tangled in the syntax and ended up with 2 faster tribbles producing 15 offspring in 7.5 hours, that is also a reasonable answer.

Game Show

Yes, it is; it doubles your chance of winning. Initially, you pick 1 of 3 with no guidance, so there is 1 chance in 3 that your box is correct. If it is not, then there are two boxes left, 1 correct and 1 incorrect, and the referee removes the incorrect box – leaving just the correct one. So if you were wrong, switching gives you 100% chance of winning. If you were right, not switching gives you 100% chance of winning. But you are only right 1 time in 3, so by switching, you increase your chance to 2 times in 3. In effect, what you are really being asked is whether your odds are better with the one box you picked, or with the two you did not. Still uncertain? Imagine there are 1,000 boxes. You pick one randomly, and the referee then discards 998 incorrect ones. Now either you luckily picked the correct box at random out of 1,000 – a tiny chance – or switching will give you the prize. The situation is exactly parallel.

Lion

The chain was fixed only to the lion. The other end was loose.

FAMILY MATTERS

Four. The brother was, of course, applicable to each sister individually.

GAV

He placed the cloth in a doorway, ends sticking out either side, and closed the door.

THE PARTY

Five. Setting aside identity, the nine attendees who are not you can be thought of as 1 to 9, where that number is the number of other members of the group that the individual has previously met. So 9 knows everyone, including 1, but 1 only knows one person – so 1 and 9 are partners. Then 8 must know everyone except 1, and 2 must know 8 and 9, but 9 is with 1, so 8 and 2 are partners. Similar logic accounts for 7 and 3, and 6 and 4. Person 5 remains, knowing 6, 7, 8, 9, and you. But there is only one person un-partnered now – you. So 5 is your partner. Person 4 knows 6, 7, 8, and 9 – and therefore not you. Ditto earlier people. But 6 knows 4, 5, 7, 8, 9 and you (they can't count themselves), and ditto later people. So you know 5, 6, 7, 8, and 9, and you, like your partner, know five people.

MILTON

Captain Kirk was immediately behind the mugato.

THE SEVENTH DOOR

If A is false, then the rooms are the same, and from the defining condition of sign A, the rooms must both contain gas. But that would make sign B a lie, which by definition makes room B the way through. So clearly sign A must be true, and thus room A is the way through. This means sign B is also true, and room B contains gas.

LIVING SPACE

Around a million. The precise answer is 2^x, where $x = 400 / 20 = 20$ – in other words, 1,048,576.

LIVING TIME

My purpose in these questions is to reinforce the necessity for methodical logic over blind intuition. A billion minutes is approximately 2,000 years – 1,901 years, 92 days, and 48 minutes, if you require precision. An Earth year is approximately 365 days, 6 hours, 9 minutes, and 9.76 seconds, or 525,969.16267 minutes. The point of this puzzle, and it's cousin, regarding generations, is to examine the degree to which the human mind tends to underestimate large sizes, particularly when presented with extraneous detail. If you got to even the same order of magnitude as the actual answers, then congratulations, you are quite unusual.

AHAB

The fallacy is post-hoc correlation, more casually known as magical thinking. Event A happens, says magical thinking, and event B happens. Therefore, event A caused event B. This is simply incorrect – as any scientist would cheerfully agree, correlation does not imply causation. Please do note that despite the term, magical thinking has nothing to do with spirituality.

IMPROBABILITY

Nowhere, everywhere, and/or anywhere. Since the interval to double speed keeps halving, at the one minute mark the ship must have broken the continuity of spacetime itself, and risen to infinite speed. Infinity by nature not measurable. Any actual point in spacetime is measurable, and thus the ship will have passed it. If the universe is finite but unbounded, as modern science theorizes, then the ship will have wrapped around all of spacetime an infinite number of times, placing it theoretically everywhere simultaneously or, possibly, arbitrarily anywhere. If the universe is finite and bounded, or infinite (bounded or otherwise), then the ship must be outside of spacetime, and the only real way of describing that is 'nowhere'. Please note that this is, of course, impossible.

FIZZBIN

The card with the number two, and the card with the black patch. These are the only ones that can falsify the proposition. The card with the white patch is irrelevant, as the propostition does not require odd numbers to have a black patch. Ditto the card bearing the number one, about which no prediction is made. However, unless the card with the number two is white and the number of the card with the black patch is odd, the proposition will be disproved.

HYDRATED

The bubbles will be drawn together. Their presence will mean that for the water between the two, there is more force pulling orthogonally away from the line connecting the two bubbles than there is pulling along that line. So the water between them will be pulled away, and the bubbles will come together.

CONTINGENT

E is definitely telling the truth. If B is lying, A, C, D, E and F are all telling the truth. If B is telling the truth, A, C, D, and F are lying, and E is telling the truth because D is not. There is no way to tell which is correct, but either way, E is telling the truth.

POLYHEDRAL

It would be even – if the single-digit numbers were included with an implicit 0 before them. As they are not, there are nine numbers missing from evenness where the second digit is larger. Thus there are more with a larger first digit.

ROSTER

Originally, the order was Chapel, Leslie, M'Benga, McCoy. After the first two switches, it became M'Benga, McCoy, Chapel, Leslie. After Leslie's schedule conflict, it became Leslie, McCoy, Chapel, M'Benga. Finally, after Chapel's collapse from exhaustion, the roster ended up as Leslie, McCoy, M'Benga, Chapel.

THE EIGHTH DOOR

If the sign reading "This room holds oblivion" belongs to door A and is lying, then by definition the room has to contain gas, which is non-consistent. If, on the other hand, it belongs to door A and is telling the truth, then again by definition it is non-consistent. So "This room holds oblivion" is sign B, and "Both rooms hold oblivion" is sign A. Sign A still cannot be true, by the chamber's definitions, so it is lying, and room A contains gas – and in order for sign A to be a lie, room B must be the way through. Room B's sign, "This room holds oblivion," also has to be a lie – which is consistent with the rules regarding that room's safety. Room B is the way forward.

GALILEO'S PARADOX

Both sets of numbers extend infinitely. Infinity is not countable; it is an idea that, whilst clearly trivially real, also cannot exist within reality. Infinity is just one place where mathematical logic tends to breaks down. So as you can see, relying on just logic and mathematics is extremely dangerous. Consciousness is required to avoid such traps, and attain genuine rationality.

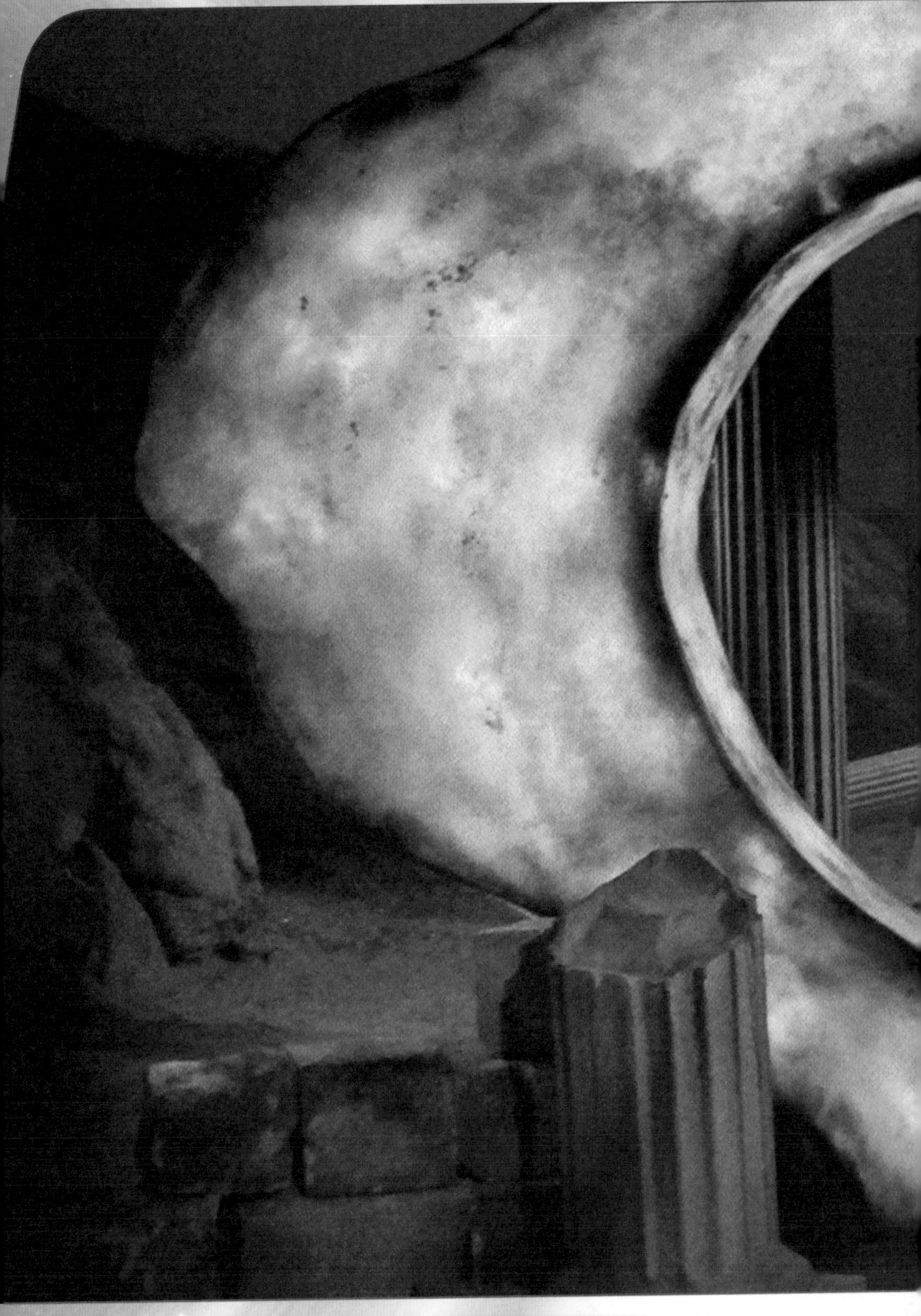

DECRYPT

The number 8549176320 has the digits 0 to 9 arranged in alphabetical order.

O.K.

Frank. Ike is drinking beer, wearing gold, and carrying a "Cavalry." Frank is drinking water, wearing blue, and carrying an "Artillery." Tom is drinking moonshine, wearing cream, and carrying a "Civilian." William is drinking sarsaparilla, wearing black, and carrying a "Gunfighter." Billy is drinking whiskey, wearing red, and carrying a "Storekeeper."

PILLS

Divide all three pills in half, setting one half of all three in one pile, and the other halves of the three in the other pile. Then remove a pill of the first type, and divide that into two, setting half of that in each of the two piles. You then have two piles of four half-pills, each of which is guaranteed to be two halves of type one, and two halves of type two. Take one pile today, and the other pile tomorrow.

PLATO'S DILEMMA

There is no way for Plato to keep his oath. Socrates's statement is simple, and easily either true or false, so whatever happens, he must accept that his oath will have to be been broken. From there, it would seem that he is under no particular onus to do anything, and thus is free to let Socrates pass, to turn him back, to throw him to his death, or, indeed, to execute him in some other manner.

DOHLMAN

Yes. If Elaan is involved, she must have had an accomplice, as she still has her dagger; if she was not involved, someone else did it. Either way, either Kryton or Durock are definitely involved. If Durock is innocent, Kryton is the attacker; if Durock is the attacker, he must have had an order from Kryton to attack. Kryton is definitely involved. In fact, it turned out that Kryton was acting alone.

LIAR

No. The error is in assuming that 'true' and 'false' are the only two states which the pronouncement can occupy. Reality is rarely either/or. The statement is neither true nor a lie – it is simply *wrong*.

THE NINTH DOOR

A. Signs B and C are mutually exclusive, so one of the two must be true. That means sign A is a lie, and Room A is actually the way through. This also means that sign B must be a lie, making sign C the true one.

BRIDGE

Start at the bottom of the deck and work backwards. Deal the last card to yourself, the second-to-last to the person on your right, and continue counter-clockwise until you run out of cards.

new dawn

After 6am. Dawn occurs when the planet rotates your location into the path of sunlight which has already arrived, so its speed makes no difference to the time you personally rotate into direct light. However, the atmosphere diffracts the light somewhat, spreading it out, so that dawn occurs slightly before you are actually in a direct line to the sun. If light moved more quickly, this diffraction effect would be reduced, so it would take longer for dawn to occur. The precise amount would be variable according to latitude, atmospheric conditions, local geography, and so on.

THE ROMULAN PROBLEM

Gardun was envious. Mikhol was violent. Tal was sadistic. Charvanek was credulous.

THEA

If there is just one unfaithful husband, every wife except his own will know of his actions. So the wife who does not know of any unfaithful husbands is the one who has been betrayed. If there are two unfaithful husbands, both their wives will know of one betrayal, so neither will execute their husband that night. When no execution happens, each will realize that there must be one more unfaithful husband, and they will execute them on the second night. If there are more than two cheating husbands, the same principle follows. Each spurned wife will be aware of n-1 cheats, and when no executions happen on day n-1, they will realize that their own husband is also a cheat.

FALSE ANGELS

Yes. Blue spirits are flickering, which means that they are not well presented, and thus cannot be false angels.

CHILDREN

Don Linden is 10 and prefers strawberry ice-cream. Tommy Starnes is 12 and prefers chocolate ice-cream. Mary Janowski is 9 and prefers vanilla ice-cream. Steve O'Connell is 11 and prefers banana ice-cream. Ray Tsing Tao is 8 and prefers caramel ice-cream.

BRAINS

On the first turn, examine a pair of diagonally opposed tumblers, and ensure both are turned upwards. On the second turn, examine two orthogonally adjacent tumblers. At least one will be up. If the other is down, turn it up as well. Assuming the test is not completed, then three tumblers are upright and one is down. On the third turn, again choose a diagonally opposite pair of tumblers. If one of them is the single down one, turn it up and finish. If they are both upright, turn one of them down, giving you two upright tumblers adjacent to each other, and two downward ones, likewise adjacent. On the fourth turn, choose two adjacent tumblers and reverse them both. If they are the same orientation, you've finished. Otherwise, this gives you two upright and two downward, this time with the pairs diagonally opposite each other. Finally, on the fifth turn, choose two diagonally opposite tumblers and invert them to guarantee all four are the same orientation.

LIONNAIS

Of course. The problem lies with the definition of the word 'interesting'. 39's status as interesting psychologically does not invalidate its status as mathematically uninteresting. Whatever mathematical yardstick Le Lionnais was using to judge the number, that evaluation will not change simply because human consciousness is easily impressed by things that break pattern.

STRIP

One of each, impossible as that seems. Despite the fact that the resulting shape, known as a Moebius strip, is fully three-dimensional, it defies commonly-accepted rules of behavior for physical objects.

Deep Nothing

The series that are being manipulated here are infinite. By its nature, infinity is uncountable – unreal – and therefore indefinite. The associative law only applies to fixed sequences. Infinite (+1-1) and (-1+1) chains are equal to each other, but not amenable to associative rearrangement.

The Tenth Door

Room B cannot be the way forward, since the way forward's room's sign needs to be true. Thus room B contains gas, and its sign is true. That leaves one room that is true and the way forward, and one that is false and lying. Sign A agrees with sign B, and thus is also true, so sign A must be on the door of the way forward, and room C must be the one that is lying and containing gas.

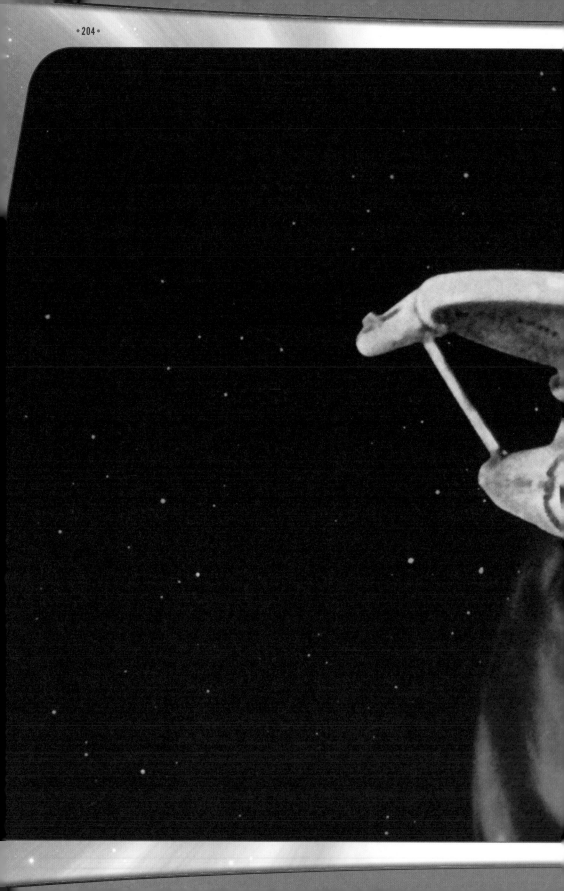

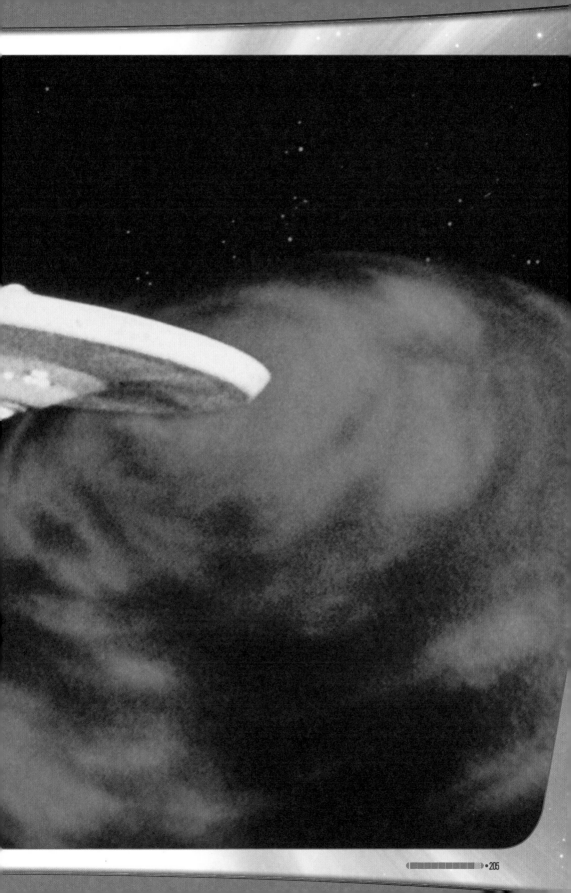

Gems

There is no way to answer correctly. Generally, a random answer to a four-possibility question gives a chance of 25%. However, B and C are both 25%, so the chance of getting a 25% answer is 50%. That means D, which is 50%, but at random, there's only a 25% chance, which makes it B or C. So that is paradoxical, and there's no chance of getting a correct answer. But 0% is A, so there's a 25% chance of getting that... which brings us back to B or C. In other words, as stated, the question is insoluble. It's no different to asking "Pick the fish from this list: Sadness of Clowns, Voidgate Epiphany, Throckmorton."

Feeding Time

No. True happiness and common sense are mutually exclusive.

RELIABILITY

If we call the three aliens X, Y and Z, then you ask X, "Is Y older than Z?," and select whichever is indicated as the younger. If X is the eldest, it will tell you the truth, you will recruit the liar. If X is in the middle, you will get either the older or the younger at random. If X is the youngest, it will lie, and you will get the honest one.

POCKETS

Six turns. The correct method is, in order, to check rooms 2, 3, 4, 2, 3, 4. First, assume the prey starts at an even room. If it is 2, it is caught immediately. If it starts at 4, it either goes to 3, and is caught on turn 2, or to 5, and then back to 4, to be caught on turn 3. Now, assume it starts in an odd room. After two turns, it can still be in any odd room, depending on where it started. But after three turns, it has to be in an even room. Then the same logic from the first pass of 2, 3, 4 applies, and it must be caught in a maximum of six turns.

DEFIANT

At 43, Captain Warfield was the oldest. He died of a snapped neck. Lieutenant Malgarini, 23, was poisoned. Ensign Wong, 28, was killed by phaser fire. Crewman Sussman, 33, was throttled. Officer Ward, 38, was stabbed.

yonada

The old man's home was mobile, and attached to his vehicle. He'd taken the whole thing to his new destination.

T'SENG

July 16h. Soss knows that Del can't know T'seng's birthday. That implies that the month of her birthday has no candidate days of the month that are unique to that month. The days 7, 19, 18, 9, 12, 11, 13, and 10 each only occur once. So the birthday has to be in July or August. This confirms the precise date for Del. Both July and August have candidates of 14, so it can't be that. The remaining possible dates are July 16, August 15, or August 17. But Del's declaration gives Soss the knowledge he needs. That means it must be a month with only one candidate number remaining. T'seng's birthday is July 16.

RAGE

They were walking on the spot, for the purpose of exercise – although the ambler was clearly half-hearted. If you thought of some other means by which a person may walk without progressing anywhere, such as a treadmill, that is also perfectly acceptable.

THE ELEVENTH DOOR

The way forward bears a true sign. If sign C is true, it does pave the way forward. So the way forward is not through door C. If the sign on door B is true, then room B is the way through, and room A contains gas, leaving room C as imprisonment. But sign A would then also be true – in fact, all three signs would be true – so sign B must be false. Thus, by elimination room A is is the way through, and its sign true. Room C contains imprisonment, and its sign is also true. Room B contains gas, and its sign is false.

PLAY

My statements that I am not guilty, and that the Captain's accusations are a lie, are consistent. Since I only get one lie, they must be true, and my accusation of Nurse Chapel is the lie. So she and I are innocent. Lieutenant Uhura and Captain Kirk both accuse me, using up their lies, so they are innocent, and Lieutenant Uhura really doesn't know Nurse Chapel (within the bounds of this question, that is). Thus Nurse Chapel's assertion that she knows Lieutenant Uhura is her lie, and Dr. McCoy is guilty, his lie being his protestation of innocence.

GRANDIOSITY

They were not playing against each other. Logical thinking requires an awareness of the danger of assumption.

SPEEDY

As it is of no concern in which order the balls are selected, there are 10 possible pairs of balls that one can draw from a pool a five. Of those, seven pairs contain at least one red, but only one of the seven contains both reds. The chance is therefore 1/7th. The chance of a second red would be 1/4 only if I had drawn out one ball, declared it red, and then drawn a second ball – but I drew them both, and am assessing two balls rather than one.

scalos

It has been established that the value of your fortune will increase more quickly than world hunger. Thus, eventually, there will come a day when you have sufficient funds to eliminate all global hunger. Logically, you would act on that day. It is also reasonable to wait a little longer, until you had that required sum plus your original fortune, to then set towards some other charitable goal.

black
and white

The last in line cannot improve his chances beyond 50%, but he can ensure the others survive. The group agree, in advance of the trial, that if the person at the end can see an odd number of white marks, he'll say "white," and if it is an even or zero number of white marks, he'll say "black." If the person in front hears "white" and sees an odd number of white marks as well, then she knows her mark is black. If she sees an even number of white marks, then hers is white as well. The obverse holds true if the last person says "black." The rest of the line, hearing the first declaration, will know whether there are an even or odd number of white marks in the nine – and, every time they hear "white" again, they'll know that the number of white marks has flipped between odd and even. From that, they can use similar logic to extricate themselves. So the group ensures 90% survival for certain, with a 50% chance of 100% survival.

LAST PASS

The likelihood is 50%. The irrational person might resolve the situation by choosing to sit in either the first seat or the last seat – both possibilities being equally likely – or, if not, he sits in some other seat. If he sits in some other seat, everything is normal until another passenger finds their seat taken, at which point she becomes the de facto irrational person – and the same logic applies. Whenever you hit the resolution stage, the person who resolves it has a 50/50 chance of leaving the last passenger's seat free. If you require a mathematical proof, consider that the problem stops when someone sits in the first seat. The chance of that ranges from 1/100 (irrational) to 1/1 (last person if all others taken). The overall probability is a summation of $(1/n(n+1))$, from n=100 to 1; this returns 0.5.

THE TWELFTH DOOR

If room H holds imprisonment, the statement on sign H about door I becomes impossible to assess, leaving the whole structure unsolvable. But since knowing H would make it solvable, it does not hold imprisonment. Sign H rules room H out of safety, since the safe room has a true sign. Thus room H contains gas, and sign H is false. Since one of sign H's conditions is that the room contains gas, it is the other condition that must be false. Door I does not lead to imprisonment. Like H, if I was safe, its sign is contradictory, so I also contains gas, and when it says that sign F is false, it is lying. So sign F is true, and sign C must be false. For sign C to be false, sign E must be false, and sign G true. From E, signs B and D are false. This means sign A is true. Sign A reduces options to doors A, C, E, G, and I. We know that doors C, E and I have false signs, and so are not the way forward. So doors A and G are the remaining possibilities. Sign G is true, and says that room A is not safe, so G is the correct door.

memory alpha

It is completely certain. Any three points on a spherical surface must, of necessity fall within one arbitrarily-placed hemisphere. Two points permit a straight line, and if this is assigned as the hemisphere boundary, then clearly the third point must either fall in one hemisphere or the other.

ardana

At the very centre of the planet.

VS. MASON
HEAVYWEIGHTS
SEMI-MAIN EVENT
6 ROUNDS
WILL
VS. BAILEY
HEAVYWEIGHTS
PRELIMINARIES
4 ROUNDS
VS. KILLER KIDD
MULANEY VS. GUS BARNES
VS. RICKY MASON
$2.50 - GENERAL ADMISSION

LITTLE MINDS

That Dr. Sevrin is either lying, deluded, insane or a combination of the three. There is no combination by which his accusations can be self-consistent.

FRICTION

By using the atmosphere. If you had some possessions, you could throw them away to drive yourself in the opposite direction, but you do not. However, when you inhale, air comes into your mouth from every available angle, producing very little force, but when you exhale, the breath is focussed. If you blew firmly, you would give yourself some momentum away from the direction you were breathing in. Re-filling your lungs would not cancel this out.

PARANOIDS

The historian padlocks the box and sends it to his colleague. The colleague then padlocks the box a second time, with an equally sturdy lock of his own, and sends it back. The first historian receives the double-locked box and removes his own lock, then hands the box back for delivery to his colleague, who can unlock the last lock.

ZARABETH

It would stay where it was, unmoving. Designating the direction to the nearest part of the sphere as forwards, whilst the nearest spot would pull the ball forwards harder, there would be more points pulling it backwards. The two forces balance precisely at every point inside the sphere.

FINALE

Five of them are true, and the other five are false. The general rule in formulations like this is that an odd total number of statements is insoluble, but if the total number is even, a half-half split is the only self-consistent possibility. If you consider the case where there are just two statements, the logic should become obvious.